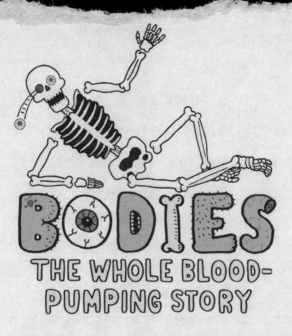

BODIES
THE WHOLE BLOOD-PUMPING STORY

Glenn Murphy wrote his first book, *Why Is Snot Green?*, while working at the Science Museum, London. Since then he has written around twenty popular-science titles aimed at kids and teens, including the bestselling *How Loud Can You Burp?* and *Space: The Whole Whizz-Bang Story*.

These days he lives in ~~North~~ Carolina – with his ~~wife, son and~~ two *unfeasibly large* ~~cats.~~

D0893169

SPACE: THE WHOLE WHIZZ-BANG STORY

SUPERGEEK! DINOSAURS, BRAINS AND SUPERTRAINS

SUPERGEEK! ROBOTS, SPACE AND FURRY ANIMALS

WHY IS SNOT GREEN?
And other extremely important questions
(and answers) from the Science Museum

HOW LOUD CAN YOU BURP?
And other extremely important questions
(and answers) from the Science Museum

STUFF THAT SCARES YOUR PANTS OFF!
The Science Museum Book of Scary Things
(and ways to avoid them)

DOES FARTING MAKE YOU FASTER?
And other extremely important questions (and answers)
about sport from the Science Museum

WILL FARTS DESTROY THE PLANET?
And other extremely important questions (and answers)
about climate change from the Science Museum

POO! WHAT *IS* THAT SMELL?
Everything you ever needed to know about the five senses

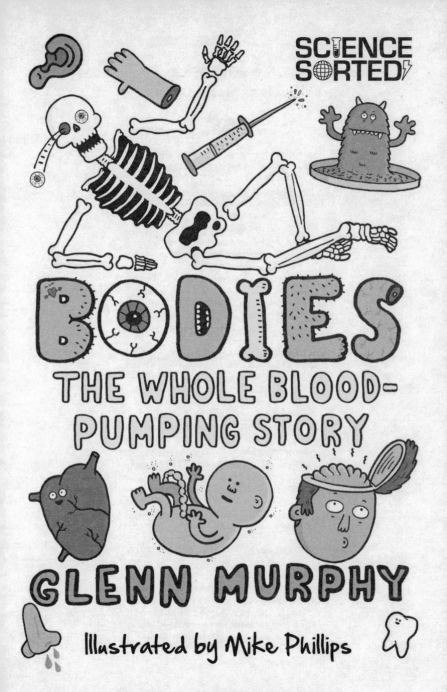

SCIENCE SORTED

BODIES
THE WHOLE BLOOD-PUMPING STORY

GLENN MURPHY

Illustrated by Mike Phillips

MACMILLAN CHILDREN'S BOOKS

*For Heather and Sean, who learned a lot about their bodies
(and bodily functions) this year*

Some material in this book has previously been published in 2011
by Macmillan Children's Books in *Brains, Bodies, Guts and Stuff*

This edition published 2014 by Macmillan Children's Books
a division of Macmillan Publishers Limited
20 New Wharf Road, London N1 9RR
Basingstoke and Oxford
Associated companies throughout the world
www.panmacmillan.com

ISBN 978-1-4472-5459-1

Text copyright © Glenn Murphy 2011, 2014
Illustrations copyright © Mike Phillips 2011, 2014
Design and doodles: Dan Newman

The right of Glenn Murphy and Mike Phillips to be identified as the
author and illustrator of this work has been asserted by them
in accordance with the Copyright, Designs and Patents Act 1988.

135798642

A CIP catalogue record for this book is available from the British Library.

Printed and bound by CPI Group (UK) Ltd, Croydon CRO 4YY

CONTENTS

HOW TO BUILD A BODY

Okay, so let's imagine that you want to build a human body . . .

What, out of bits of dead people? Like Frankenstein or something?

No, not like that. You're not allowed to use whole arms, legs and heads. They're already half-built, aren't they? I meant a whole human body, built from *scratch*. Where would you start?

Hmmm . . . let's see. I s'pose I'd start with a skeleton. I'd wire a bunch of bones together, like they do with dinosaur bones in museums, and make a skeleton.

That's a good start. But a skeleton can't stand up or move by itself. You can dangle it from a hook to stop it collapsing into a heap of bones, but that's about it. How are you going to get it standing and moving?

Easy. I strap some muscles on there. String 'em between all the bones, so they can hold the skeleton up and pull the arms and legs about. Oh, and then cover the whole lot with skin, so it doesn't look too hideous.

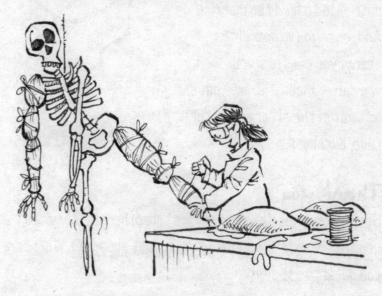

Nice work. This body is really starting to take shape. But here's the thing — if those muscles are going to do any work at all, they'll need *energy*. Where are you going to get that?

Ah. Good point. Right, then – we stick in a stomach and some guts, so it can digest food and get energy from that. Oh, and stick some teeth in the gob, so it can mash the food up.
And a food tube, I s'pose, to get food from the mouth to the stomach.

Great idea. So now you've got a **digestive tube** for absorbing nutrients to feed the muscles. And, once you've got all the energy you can from your food, you can – ahem – 'drop' what's left out of the other end of the tube. Excellent.

Thank you.

But working muscles need oxygen too, otherwise they can't use the chemical food-energy you've just absorbed. Where are you going to get that?

Easy – shove some lungs in. And some air tubes leading to the nose and mouth. Sorted.

Not quite.

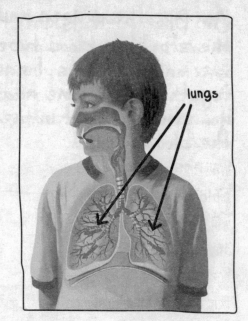

lungs

Eh? (Sigh) What now?

Now you have two lungs full of oxygen, and a gut full of chemical energy from your food. But how are you going to get the oxygen and energy to muscles spread all over your body, from head to toe?

Oh, yeah. Hmmmm . . . tricky one, that. Hang on . . . got it!

On you go . . .

You pipe the oxygen and energy there in little blood tubes! You link all the muscles, guts, lungs and stuff together with veins and arteries. Then you stick a heart in the middle to pump the blood around.

Well done. You've created a **bloodstream**, which will now carry oxygen and energy all over the body – a brilliant solution. But there's still a problem. What's going to keep the whole system working together? How are you going to *coordinate* and *control* all this eating, breathing, pumping and moving about?

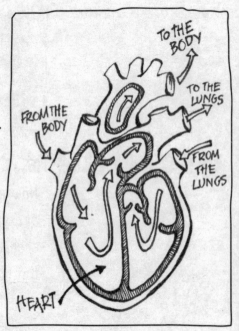

TO THE BODY

TO THE LUNGS

FROM THE BODY

FROM THE LUNGS

HEART

Doh! Of course! I forgot the brain! Okay – here's what we do. We shove a brain in the skull to control everything, and we wire it up to all the body bits we already have with nerves. Oh, and while we're about it let's stick some eyeballs and eardrums in the head too. And wire up the nose, mouth and skin so they can smell, taste and touch things. Howzat?

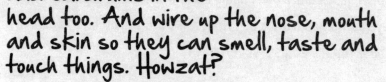

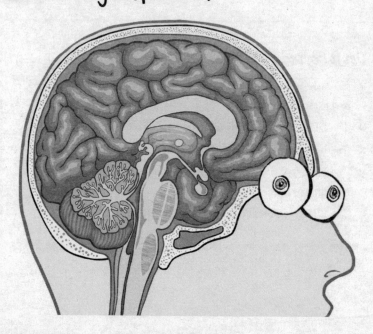

A masterstroke. Now your body can control itself and get information about the outside world through your five senses of sight, sound, touch, taste and smell. (And, as a bonus, your brain also lets you think and learn about stuff as you go.) We're nearly there.

Nearly?

Yep, nearly. Just a couple more things to deal with, and we're done. Now think hard, because this next one's a biggie.

You've just built a body using most of the major **organ systems** needed for life. Now, what are you going to build all these organs and systems out of?

Get It Sorted – The Major Organ Systems

* The movement (or MUSCULOSKELETAL) system is made of bones and muscles.
* The DIGESTIVE system absorbs energy.
* The breathing (or RESPIRATORY) system absorbs oxygen.
* The blood (or CIRCULATORY) system moves the oxygen and energy around.
* The BRAIN and NERVOUS SYSTEM controls the whole lot.

Errr . . . what?

Well, so far you've built a muscly skeleton, skin, guts, lungs, blood vessels, nerves, eyes, ears, a heart and a brain. What will you actually use to build these body organs? Wood? Plasticine? Lego? What?

Oh. Wow. I . . . errr . . . never thought about that. Well, bones are made of bone, aren't they? And muscles are made of . . . well . . . muscle?

That's right, they are. But it goes a bit deeper than that. In biology, we call these organ-building materials *tissues*. Most tissues are made of stringy protein fibres, fatty membranes and watery, sugary gels. Some special tissues, like bone tissue, also contain minerals like calcium, to make them tougher and stronger.

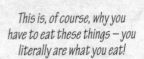

This is, of course, why you have to eat these things – you literally are what you eat!

What's that?

Now your body is *delicious* and *nutritious*. But proteins, fats and sugars aren't just good grub for us. They're also good grub for bacteria and other microscopic parasites – which just love to invade your body and munch away on your yummy tissues. Before long, your precious body will be chewed up, rotten and decayed. So how are you going to stop them?

Wrap yourself in cling film? Take some antibiotics?

Okay, not bad. In a way, your *skin* acts like cling film – covering your delicate, watery tissues with a protective layer that stops bacteria getting in. And while your body doesn't make antibiotics, it does make antibodies and other bacteria-busting defence systems, which lie in the tissues and bloodstream, waiting to do battle.

11

But even with all these defences your tissues will eventually break down by themselves. Just as cogs, wheels, circuits and pipes wear out inside machines, so too do your bones, joints, muscles, nerves and blood tubes. How are you going to fix that?

Errr . . . repair them? Or replace the worn-out parts with new ones?

Excellent. That's exactly what we'll do. In fact, we'll go one better. We'll make the tissues repair and regenerate themselves. As old parts wear down, we'll grow new parts to replace them.

We can do that? How?

By building our tissues out of living, growing, regenerating **cells**.

Get It Sorted – Cells

Cells are the most basic building blocks of life. The tissues of your body may be made of proteins, fats and sugars, but they're organized into tissues by layers of cells. Muscle tissue is built with layers of muscle cells, bone tissue with bone cells, brain and nerve tissue with nerve cells. And so on.

But don't cells wear out too?

Most of them do, yes. But cells also grow and divide, replacing layers of old, dead cells in a tissue with fresh, new ones from beneath.

In the absence of a nasty disease or accident, the whole process keeps your body ticking along for decades, with no mechanic, plumber or electrician required. Let's see any other machine top that!

So that's it, then? We've done it? We've built a body?

Yep – we're done.

Hooray! We rule!

Good job. We now have a living, breathing, moving body that can take care of itself. We've used cells to build tissues, tissues to build organs and organs to build organ systems. Now just add food, water and oxygen, and you're away!

Now you're ready to explore the really *good* stuff. On our tour of the human body we'll discover why we faint, why we get dizzy and why we have toes. We'll find out how tummies rumble, how karate masters chop through concrete, and how you could live with half a brain.

You ready, Dr Frankenstein?

Yeah! Let's do it!

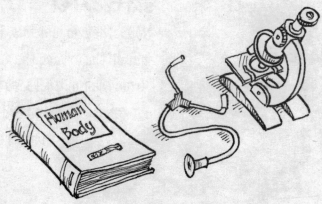

BLOOD, BREATH AND BODY PUMPS

How do babies breathe before they're born?

They don't. Because they don't have to. While they're in the womb, their mothers do their breathing for them. And while babies do 'practise' breathing in the womb, they don't take their first breath until they're pushed out into the cold, airy world.

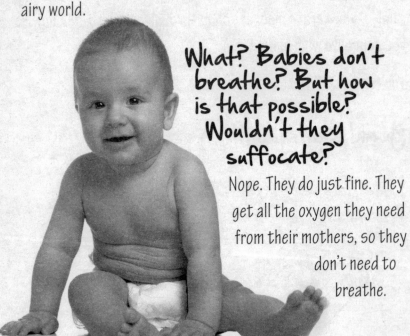

What? Babies don't breathe? But how is that possible? Wouldn't they suffocate?

Nope. They do just fine. They get all the oxygen they need from their mothers, so they don't need to breathe.

At least not until they're out of the womb and the **umbilical cord** that connects them to their mothers is cut.

So they breathe through that tube? Like a snorkel or something?

In a manner of speaking, yes. Only they're not actually breathing. They're just receiving oxygen through the cord, and making use of it.

I don't get it. If you stop breathing, you die. Everybody knows that.

Ah, but that's not strictly true, you see. At least not for everybody, all the time. Think about it — how long can you hold your breath?

I dunno – about a minute?

Right. And did you die last time you tried?

17

Don't be stupid. If I did, I couldn't say so, could I?

Exactly. So you stopped breathing for a full minute and yet here you are, alive and well.

Eh? So you're saying that babies hold their breath? For, like, nine months?

No, no, no, no, no. Not at all. I'm saying that you don't necessarily have to be breathing to be receiving and using oxygen. That's because there's a big difference between **breathing** (moving air in and out of your lungs) and **respiration** (using oxygen from your bloodstream to power your brain and other tissues). If you stop respiring, your cells cannot use oxygen to power themselves, and you die. But you can stop **breathing** for several minutes before you stop **respiring**. That's why you can hold your breath without dying. What's more, if you can find another way to get oxygen into your bloodstream, then you don't need to breathe at all.

So how do babies do it?

For the nine months that it's inside the womb, a baby (or rather, the **foetus**, which is the correct word for a developing baby before it is born) receives oxygen through the **umbilical cord**. This fleshy cord is made up of three thick blood vessels (two **umbilical arteries** and one **umbilical vein**). The umbilical vein passes into the foetus's belly (where the belly button will eventually be), and carries nutrients and fresh oxygen to the baby's liver and heart. On the return route, carbon dioxide and other wastes are carried from the baby's hip (or iliac) arteries, up past the bladder and back out through the belly into the umbilical veins. In this way, oxygen and nutrients pass in and out of the body of the growing foetus without it ever having to breathe (or, for that matter, eat).

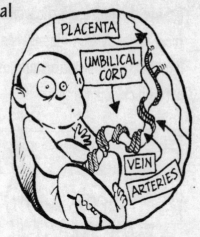

So where does the umbilical cord come from? From the mother's blood?

Not directly, no. Mixing the mother's blood and the baby's blood would be dangerous, as it could expose the foetus to all sorts of viruses, bacteria or toxic chemicals, against which it has no defence. So, instead, blood vessels from the mother and from the foetus meet inside the womb, within a special organ called the **placenta**. The placenta is formed from the same fertilized egg the foetus developed from, and it floats beside the foetus in the womb. Inside the placenta, capillaries from the mother's bloodstream and from the foetus's umbilical cord twine around each other like a pair of hands with interlacing fingers.

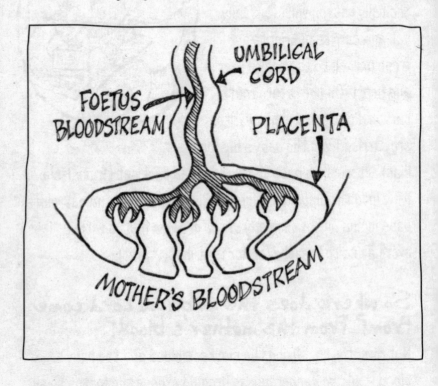

Arranged in this way, oxygen and nutrients can move back and forth through the spaces between the two bloodstreams without them ever actually flowing into each other. So the placenta works like a fleshy sieve, filtering out any nasties before they get into the umbilical cord and the foetus's blood. Which is pretty nifty, if you think about it.

So the baby doesn't use its lungs at all?

Not really, no. Right up until it's born, the foetus's lungs are filled with fluid. From about three months onwards, it makes small breathing movements with the lungs. But it's not really using the lungs to breathe with at all – it's just preparing the breathing muscles for use later on. Like a breathing 'workout' inside the womb.

But if the lungs were filled with fluid, wouldn't the baby drown when it tried to use them?

Well spotted. It *would*, but it *doesn't*. Right after the baby is pushed out of the womb, it gives a mighty heave, coughs up all the fluid, and starts breathing with its first cry.

Doctors, nurses and midwives sometimes hold the baby upside down and pat it gently on the back to help kick-start this first breath once the baby is delivered.

That's why the first thing the baby does is cry. Well — that, and because it's chilly and scary out in the big, bad world.

Wow. That's kind of amazing. Okay – one more thing. What happens to the umbilical cord and the placenta?

Once the baby is born and breathing for itself, the umbilical cord starts to shrivel up. If left alone, it would eventually break off all by itself, but in practice doctors usually clamp it and cut it a few centimetres from the baby's belly to speed this process up. The rest of it is pulled back inside the baby's abdominal cavity, to form the belly button.

As for the placenta, that pops out — attached to the other end of the umbilical cord — right after the baby. Usually the nurses just throw it away, but sometimes the parents decide to keep it as a souvenir.

Ewwww! That's gross!!

You think that's icky? Some parents even . . . No, I shouldn't say. It's probably too much for you.

What? Come on, tell me. What could be worse than keeping it as a souvenir?

Okay, you asked for it. Some parents fry it up and eat it.

BLEURRRGH!

Why do big cuts need stitches?

Because although your skin has an amazing ability to repair itself, wide or deep cuts take much longer to heal. Stitches help to hold the edges of the wound together, and keep the wound sealed off to nasty bacteria while your body gets to work patching you up.

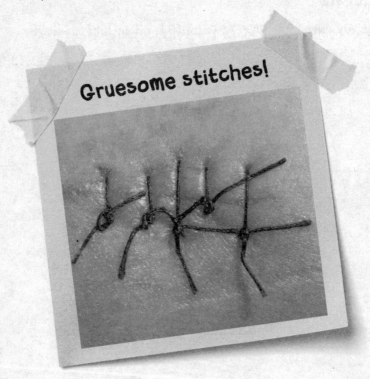

Gruesome stitches!

Warning! Gory bit

Not really, no. Usually all the bleeding has stopped by the time the surgeon or nurse starts to stitch the edges of a wound together. If it *hasn't* stopped, then stitching you up won't do much good anyway, as you'll continue to bleed into the muscles and other tissues beneath the skin. Even with no blood leaking from your body, you could still bleed to death as the blood leaks and pools inside your leg or stomach and fails to reach your brain.

But if you get a little cut, your skin heals up all by itself. So why do only bigger cuts need stitches?

What do you mean?

25

Well, let's say I'm at home playing with my cat, and she scratches me on the back of the hand. How does it work?

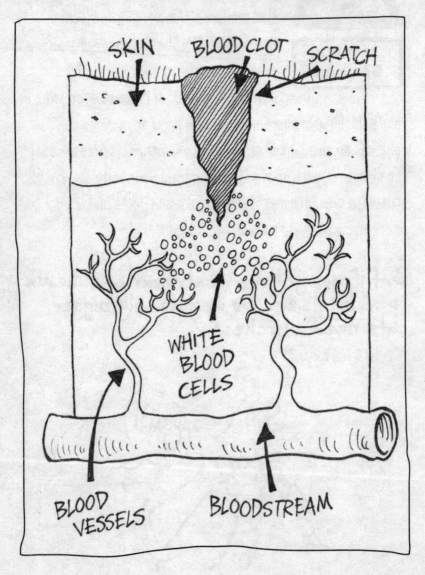

SKIN

BLOOD CLOT

SCRATCH

WHITE
BLOOD
CELLS

BLOOD
VESSELS

BLOODSTREAM

Well, as soon as your kitty's claws separate the skin, your body senses the injury, and blood vessels close to the wound shrink up to slow blood flow to the area. Then a blood clot quickly forms and plugs the small gap across the scratch. Once the bleeding has stopped, the clot then turns into one or more scabs, which appear on your skin as dark, crusty lines. Beneath the scabs, the blood vessels open again to allow bacteria-busting white blood cells to move from the bloodstream into the broken tissues of the scratch. They kill all the bacteria, and the scabs start to change colour as dead bacteria and blood cells beneath them pile up.

Get It Sorted – Haemophilia

Haemophilia is a hereditary (meaning you are born with it) blood disorder in which the blood fails to form complete clots, or forms clots less easily than it should. This puts people who suffer from the disease – called haemophiliacs – in great danger when they are injured. For a haemophiliac, even very light bumps and falls can cause bleeding beneath the skin – especially into joints. And if they're badly hurt, such as breaking a leg on the football pitch or breaking ribs in a car crash, then their internal injuries can be life-threatening.

Warning! Gory bit

What happens after that?

After that, special cells deep within your skin, called **fibroblasts**, start to multiply and grow from each side of the cut towards the middle, forming a new layer of skin beneath the scab. If all goes well, the new skin will be fully formed within a day or two, and the scabs will fall off to reveal clean, fresh skin and no trace at all of your mean kitty's scratches.

Okay. So now let's say I'm at the zoo. A huge tiger escapes, and he comes running right at me . . .

O-kay . . .

. . . at the last second, I hold up my backpack, hoping he'll prefer the sausage sandwiches in my lunch box to eating me alive.

Rrrrrooowwwl!

He swipes it out of my hands, and I run away. But his claws have sliced a massive, nasty cut right along the length of my arm, and it's gushing blood all over the place. NOW what?

Well, that's all very dramatic – if a little scary.

Thank you. I try my best. So what happens now?

Well, obviously a deep gash carved out by a tiger's claw won't heal up nearly as easily as a little swipe from Tiddles. This time the cut will go through more layers of skin, probably into the fibrous tissue and muscle below. And the gap it creates can't easily be plugged and bridged by blood clots and fibroblasts. Presuming that you made it to a hospital, or got some emergency medical help, the doctor or paramedic would try to stop the bleeding by binding the arm tightly with bandages that press down hard on to the cut. This pressure might create a temporary clot and, just as before, the blood vessels near the wound would shrink up (or constrict) to slow blood loss from the area. But, left as it is, this bigger, deeper wound would probably not heal by itself.

Why not?

Well, the clot – if it formed at all – would probably fall apart as soon as you removed the bandages to clean the wound, and you would continue bleeding. And even if another clot formed, it wouldn't hold for long. With too big a gap across the wound, the fibroblasts that make new skin and

*If you **didn't** remove the bandages, bacteria from the air (or the tiger's claws) would grow beneath them and infect the wound.*

muscle tissue would be unable to meet in the middle and seal off the wound. So clots and scabs would keep breaking up and falling out of the wound. The gash would ooze blood and pus, and eventually it would become infected by bacteria. Before long your whole arm would be infected, and surgeons would have to remove it to stop the bacteria infecting the rest of your body and killing you.

Warning! Gory bit

Nasty!

Yep. So to avoid this – and to give your body a hand with the healing process – a doctor would remove the bandages, clean the wound with anti-bacterial chemicals, bring the edges of the wound together and finally sew (or staple) them up. With less of a gap to bridge, the blood clots and scabs should hold for longer, buying enough time for the fibroblasts to regrow new tissue underneath.

Then it'd heal up again? Good as new?

No, not quite. With a deeper cut and a wider gap to bridge, the fibroblasts have to use emergency repair tactics to make sure it holds together. So instead of new skin tissue – complete with nerves, blood vessels, hair follicles and sweat glands – they weave the wound together with dense mats of a tough protein called collagen. What's left

is a patch of pale, hairless, dead-feeling **scar tissue**. This patch of your arm would never tan or sweat beneath the sun, and would look different from the rest of your skin for life. But hey — at least you didn't get infected. Or eaten.

All right, what if you were attacked by a ninja assassin – Hiiiiiyyyaaa!!! and he chopped your arm right off?

That would be tougher. If you could stop the bleeding, pick up your arm and get straight to a hospital, there would be a chance that a surgeon could reattach it. This is much easier to do with fingers and toes than entire arms or legs. But this has been done many times before (not so much the

ninja attack — I mean people getting limbs chopped off by harvesting machines and having them reattached — stuff like that). And although it leaves lots of scar tissue, sometimes people can keep using the arm for life afterwards.

What about if your whole head got chopped off?

Well . . . even if a surgeon could stop the bleeding and reattach your head with an operation (which, at present, is pretty much impossible), it would take hours to do it. And since your brain can't survive for more than a few minutes without a blood supply, I wouldn't fancy your chances.

Oh. So I should definitely avoid angry tigers and ninjas, then.

Yes. I'd say that was good advice, anyway . . .

Puzzle: Blood-clot Boggle

Now you're an expert on blood clots, try this jumbled-up picture-puzzle. In your head, assemble the five pictures in the correct order, so that when you read them from left to right, you have a comic strip telling the story of how blood clots are created. What order do the pictures appear in?

Check your answers on page 152.

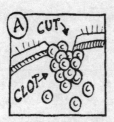

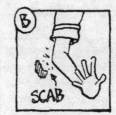

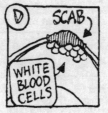

Answer: __ __ __ __ __

Why do some people faint at the sight of blood?

Fainting happens when your blood pressure drops quickly and the brain is suddenly starved of oxygen. People may 'pass out' for all kinds of reasons, including pain, hunger, fear or poor blood circulation. But fainting at the sight of blood may be an ancient reflex that prevents you from bleeding to death.

Get It Sorted – Passing Out vs. Knockouts

PASSING OUT	KNOCKED OUT
Sudden drop in blood pressure and/or oxygen supply to the brain	Head is hit and the brain is shaken, rattled or crushed against the inside of the skull causing temporary damage
Brain shuts down non-essential parts	
You lose consciousness and fall down as skeletal muscles are deactivated	
Brain in 'sleep mode' so that it can survive longer without blood/oxygen	Brain attempts emergency repairs
Unlikely to result in any brain damage	Some brain damage usually occurs

✳ Being knocked out is a response to actual brain damage
✳ Passing out is a response to the threat of brain damage

But what could make your blood pressure drop like that?

Well, there are two ways it can happen.

1 When the total volume of blood in your body decreases for some reason. If you severed a limb or an artery, this would happen quite quickly as blood came pumping out of your body. But your total blood volume can drop even without any bleeding. If you don't eat or drink for a day or two, your blood pressure drops as you gradually use up water in your body, losing it through sweat, tears, breath (as water vapour), urine and faeces. Within three to five days, your blood volume and pressure will drop low enough to make you pass out, repeatedly. And if you don't find water fast then eventually you won't wake up at all.

2 Blood – at least temporarily – fails to reach your brain. This might happen through fear, pain or at the sight of blood, not because you've suddenly lost lots of blood.

The average adult has about 4 – 7 litres of blood in their body. Losing just 1–2 litres would be enough to make most people pass out (losing 2.5 litres or more would be enough to kill you).

Eh? I don't get it. How?

Think of it this way. Imagine that your body is a big, plastic water bottle, filled to the top with lovely, red blood.

O-kayyyy . . .

Now, in order to stay conscious, the blood has to touch the cap at the top (your brain). This is fine as long as you're all topped up. But obviously, if you make a hole in the bottle, the liquid level will soon drop away from the cap (or brain) and you will pass out. A large hole will do this quickly, but making tiny pinholes

to 'pee' or 'sweat' the liquid out will eventually have the same effect, right?

But what if, when the blood couldn't quite reach the top, you were allowed to squeeze the sides of the bottle, making the volume of the blood-holding vessel smaller?

38

Well, then the blood would be squeezed up the neck of the bottle, and it'd still touch the cap.

Exactly. And this, in a way, is what blood vessels do inside your body. By keeping the volume of the container small, they keep the pressure up, and make sure that enough blood still reaches the brain up top.

But when you experience a sudden pain or fear, your body may respond by slowing your heart rate and widening the blood vessels in many parts of your body. This takes the 'squeeze' off the sides of the 'bottle', and your blood drops away from your brain to pool up in your legs. While some pressure remains in the upper body, it's not enough to feed the brain. So it responds by passing out, or fainting. This lays you out flat, so the blood can flow sideways (rather than upwards) and more easily reach your brain. Like turning our water-filled bottle on its side, so that the water swishes towards the cap under gravity alone.

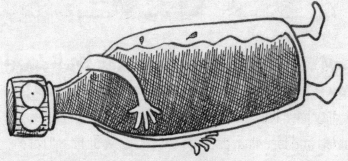

But what good would that do you if you were scared or in pain?

Well, this 'pass-out' reflex may have evolved to help you 'play dead' when suddenly attacked by a much stronger animal. The idea is that the attacker may then just ignore you, and you live to fight another day. This is called the **vasovagal response**, and people can be more or less sensitive to it. So some people faint at the slightest pain or surprise, while others can endure incredible amounts of pain or shock before passing out.

Okay . . . I get that, I s'pose. But what about fainting at the sight of blood?

That may have once been a self-defence reflex too. If you're wounded and bleeding, passing out drops your heart rate and keeps you still. This helps slow the flow of blood from the wound, buying time for your blood to form a clot. Of course, that's only helpful if it's *you* that's bleeding. Passing out at the sight of *someone else's* blood is a pretty useless response, and mostly happens in people whose vasovagal responses are too sensitive. So the same folks who pass out easily when surprised or hurt are also likely to be floored by seeing you cut your finger.

Game: Pass-Out

Grab some plasticine and a plastic water bottle, and you can simulate passing out for yourself. Here's how you do it:

1   Grab a plastic bottle and fill it almost to the top with water.

2   Grab a ball of plasticine and sculpt a self-portrait (just the head, not the whole body).

3   For dramatic effect add a few drops of red food colouring to each bottle.

4   Put the cap on the bottle and stick the plasticine head on top.

5   Squeeze the sides of your bottle until the liquid touches the top. All the time there is liquid touching the cap, your 'head' is supplied with blood and you stay conscious. If you let go of the bottle, the pressure drops and your bottle person will faint.

Which works harder, your heart or your brain?

That kind of depends on whether you're busy thinking or busy exercising. Your heart works up to three times harder during exercise, but in the long run, your brain probably tips it. Because even when you're sitting still your brain is using twice as much energy as your heart, and it takes four to five times as much blood to feed it.

You mean your heart and brain actually eat blood? Like vampires or something?

Errr . . . not quite. It's more like they eat oxygen and glucose. All your organs do. Blood is just the conveyor belt that

42

delivers these goodies to your hungry cells, tissues and organs. Red blood cells act like oxygen postmen.

They pick up oxygen molecules in the lungs and carry them to hungry tissues throughout the body. Glucose, meanwhile, moves into your bloodstream from the digestive system, and simply dissolves into your blood, making it slightly sweet and sugary. From there, it's carried around the body and dissolves into cells wherever it's needed.

OXYGEN POSTMAN

Like the muscles and the brain?

Right. While all your tissues use oxygen and glucose, your muscles and brain are perhaps the most ravenous. At rest, your muscles use around 15 per cent of your blood flow, while your brain uses roughly 20 per cent. Your heart, too, needs about 4–5 per cent of your blood supply, just to keep pumping. Without the constant movement of blood that your heart provides, your tissues would quickly become starved of oxygen and glucose, and your oxygen-hungry brain would begin to shut down. So your heart must work hard, and tirelessly, throughout your entire life.

So how hard does your heart pump?

At an average rate of 5.2 litres per minute. In one day (twenty-four hours), your heart pumps enough blood to fill the water tanks of *four* full-sized fire engines. Over a lifetime, the average heart pumps over 180 million litres of blood, or enough to fill an ocean-going oil supertanker!

Whoa!!

It's a good thing our bodies don't leak, isn't it?

Indeed. And that's nothing. During exercise, your tissues — especially your muscles — use up oxygen and glucose much more quickly. In this state, your muscles need four or five times more blood than they did at rest, so the heart has to pump much harder and faster to meet the demand for more blood. When you're resting or sleeping, your heart beats at around sixty to a hundred times per minute. But when you're sprinting or swimming as fast as you can, your heart rate can reach 200 beats per minute or more!

In doing so, they also create waste — such as carbon dioxide and lactic acid — more quickly too.

How Fast Can My Heart Go?

The average maximum heart rate decreases with age. You can figure yours out by subtracting your age from 220. So if you're ten years old, it's around 210 beats per minute. But when you reach forty, it tops out at about 180.

Oh, come on. Then your heart HAS to be working harder than the brain, right?

For short bursts, perhaps, yes. But, if you think about it, most of us sleep for a third of our lives, and spend very little time exercising this hard. Even for Olympic athletes, it's pretty much impossible to keep that level of exercise up for more than thirty minutes, let alone all day. So over the course of your lifetime your brain wins the prize.

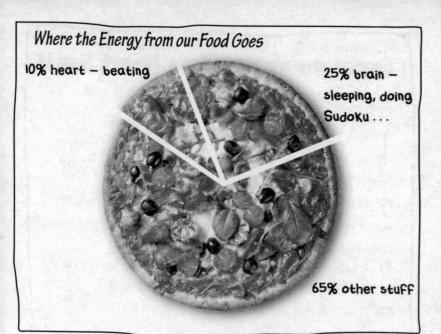

Where the Energy from our Food Goes

10% heart — beating

25% brain — sleeping, doing Sudoku...

65% other stuff

So if my teacher tells me to 'use my brain', I can just take a nap in class and leave a note stuck to my head that says 'I am!' Brilliant!

I AM BRILLIANT

Errr... you *could*, I suppose. But I wouldn't recommend it...

Experiment: See Your Heart Beat!

You don't need fancy hospital gear to see your heartbeat in action. Try this:

1   Grab a small, pea-sized blob of plasticine or clay, a stopwatch and a matchstick. Stick the matchstick most of the way through the clay blob.

2   Rest your arm, palm up, on a table in front of you. Stick the clay blob on to the inside of your wrist, just below the base of the thumb.

3   You should see the match twitch as it picks up the movement of the blood pulsing through the blood vessel beneath. If it's not moving, unstick the blob and try shifting it a little to the left or right. Got it? Good.

4   Now take the stopwatch, set it to beep after one minute, and count how many times the match twitches before it goes off. (If you don't have a stopwatch, get a friend to time it with an ordinary watch – you just count heartbeats, and your friend tells you when a minute is up.)

5   How many 'beats' did you count? The average for an adult is sixty to eighty beats per minute; for children, it's eighty to a hundred.

6   Now remove the blob and do two minutes of non-stop exercise. You can do push-ups, sit-ups, hop, skip, jump, jog on the spot – whatever. Just keeping going for two full minutes.

7   Reattach the blob and matchstick, and count the beats per minute as before.

8   How high did your heart rate go? Compare your score with your friends, and draw up a table showing your heart rates after exercise. The winner (or the fittest person) is the one with the lowest score!

Why don't lungs work underwater?

Because they didn't evolve to move liquids in and out. And, even if they could, it still wouldn't work. Water contains far less free oxygen than air, so even if your lungs could inhale and exhale water they still couldn't get enough oxygen out to sustain your big, warm-blooded body.

But there's loads of oxygen in water. I mean, fish breathe underwater, right?

Right. But fish use **gills** to do it, not lungs. Gills are thin, feathery organs adapted for underwater breathing (or rather, underwater **respiration**), which are clearly visible on either side of the head. They have a huge surface area for capturing the oxygen dissolved in water and dumping carbon dioxide back into it.

In fish respiration, water is moved past these surfaces by the movement of the gills, and the movement of the fish itself as it swims through the water.

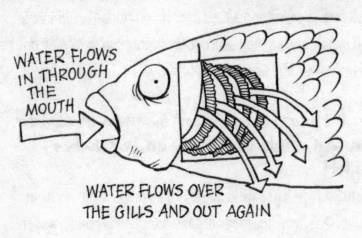

WATER FLOWS IN THROUGH THE MOUTH

WATER FLOWS OVER THE GILLS AND OUT AGAIN

Lungs, on the other hand, are found deep inside the body, further away from the oxygen source they need to get at. With each inhalation, air is sucked in through the nose or mouth and travels down your windpipe (or **trachea**). In the middle of your chest, the trachea splits into two major branches (or **bronchi**) which each enter a lung.

You have two big branches poking into your lungs? Yikes! Isn't that a bit dangerous?

Not real branches, no. More like *forks*.

What? Now you've got **cutlery** in there?

Errr . . . no. I meant 'branches' or 'forks' in the air tubes that lead into your lungs. As in 'junctions'. Okay?

Phew! That's a relief. Thought I was going to have to call an ambulance or something . . .

No, it's fine. You're fine. I'm fine. Now, where was I?

Airways?

Right. Airways. So, inside the lungs, these airways branch again and again into smaller and smaller passages called **bronchioles**. The whole thing looks a bit like an upside-down tree, with a trunk at the top and limbs and branches spreading out sideways into each lung. At the tips of these branches are tiny, berry-like sacs called **alveoli**. These sacs are lined with a thick layer of fluid, and surrounded by tiny blood vessels. Once it reaches the alveoli, oxygen from the air you inhale dissolves into the fluid inside, and oxygen and

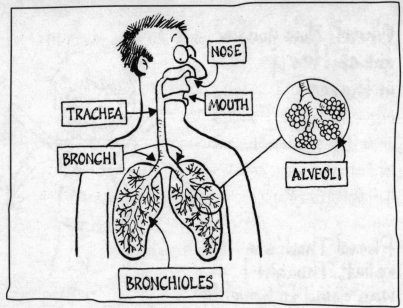

carbon dioxide are exchanged with red blood cells in the bloodstream. This done, the carbon dioxide dissolves out of the fluid, flows up through the bronchioles to the trachea, and exits the body as you exhale.

Aha! There you go, you see? The oxygen in your lungs has to dissolve into the fluid in those little lung-berry things anyway, right? So why can't you just fill your lungs with water and let the oxygen from the water dissolve straight into the blood?

Well, if your lungs do happen to fill with water — as in when you're drowning — that's exactly what does happen.

Great! But wait — why do you drown, then?

Because unfortunately there just isn't anywhere near enough oxygen in a lungful of water for your body to get by. While there is some oxygen dissolved in fresh water, compared with air, the same volume of water contains twenty times less of it. Now that may be enough to sustain a cold-blooded fish with the right gear to extract it, but it's nowhere near enough oxygen for a large warm-blooded mammal like you.

And, besides, you don't have the right gear for the job. Your lungs evolved to move light, gassy air in and out of the body. Water is much thicker and heavier than air, so — as anyone who has nearly drowned will tell you — once it gets into the lungs it's hard to shift, and it tends to stay there.

Get It Sorted — You Can't Breathe Underwater Because:

a) your lungs can't breathe water in and out, and

b) even if you could, there wouldn't be enough air in each watery breath to support your body.

Boo. That's a shame. Breathing underwater would be so cooooool.

Yes, it would. But it's a skill best left to the fishes. In the meantime, there's always snorkels and scuba gear . . .

FOOD TUBES AND PLOP GATES

STOMACH TURNING ALERT! READ ON IF YOU DARE ...

Does the colour of sick depend on what you've just eaten?

Usually, yes. Since vomit is most often simply half-digested food brought back up, its colour is usually a sloppy mix of the colourful foods you just pigged out on. But, more rarely, illness and poisoning can make your chunder go some pretty funky shades.

Top 5 words for 'sick'

Add your own favourites!

Vomit ....

Puke ....

Chunder ....

Technicolour Yawn ....

Street Pizza ....

Sick is **usually** just a mix of foods?

Usually, yes. Your average puddle of sick is most often just a sloppy mass of saliva, mucus and half-digested food, brought back up before your stomach **EEEEEWWWWW** and intestines could finish their job. If you just ate it a few minutes ago, it will probably be the exact same colour that the food started out. This might include leafy green, a meaty or chocolatey brown or the brighter shades of food colourings from – for example – the huge box of sweets you just scarfed.

But sometimes there are other things in your vomit – besides food – that may contribute to its colour too.

Other things? Like what?

Like bits of your stomach lining, brightly coloured digestive juices and – if you're really unlucky – blood.

Urrrrrrgh!

So why do we throw up anyway? Is it just to get rid of extra food when we eat too much?

That's one reason, yes. If you eat or drink too much, or too quickly for your digestive system to handle, nerves in your swollen stomach send a signal to a part of the brain called the **emetic centre**. This, in turn, triggers the muscles in your **oesophagus** (or food tube) to push some or all of the stomach's contents back up to your mouth.

Get It Sorted – What Goes Down...

When you swallow a lump of food, muscles in the wall of your oesophagus contract in downward waves, pushing the food down the throat and into the stomach. This wave-like squeezing is called peristalsis, and each successful swallow is done with its own peristaltic wave.

... Sometimes Comes Back Up

To bring your sloppy sick back up, your stomach muscles contract to help squeeze its contents up into the oesophagus. From there, it's just like swallowing in reverse. Peristalsis pushes the food upwards with a series of rising waves, until the slop reaches your mouth.

Yuck! So throwing up happens for other reasons too?

Right. While the process of 'chucking up' stays more or less the same, it can come about for lots of reasons besides overeating.

Sometimes this works and sometimes it doesn't. All these things are best avoided altogether if you don't want to throw up or be poisoned.

1 It can be a reaction to eating rotten food, toxic plants and fungi, or to drugs, alcohol and other toxic substances. If your digestive system detects these, your brain may trigger vomiting to help clear the poisons and toxins from the body.

2 It could be to clear the throat of trapped objects and prevent choking. This is called gagging, and it's triggered by the **gag reflex** (also called the **pharyngeal reflex**). Interestingly one-third of people have no gag reflex at all, while others are so sensitive that they gag every time a toothbrush touches the roof of their mouth.

3 It can be a symptom of disease, and is often a sign of infection by viruses or bacteria.

4 It can be triggered by fear, nervousness or anxiety. The effect can be anything from 'butterflies in the tummy' to queasiness to full-on puking. Which is no fun at all when you're playing the lead part in the school play.

Get It Sorted – Diarrhoea

Bad food can also give you diarrhoea because it's filled with nasty microbes that affect your guts, making the lining swell up and preventing it from absorbing water from your poo. The result is what's medically known as diarrhoea (or more commonly known as the runs or the trots).

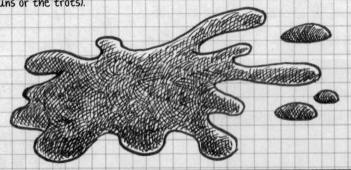

Microbes like this grow inside all types of food, and any food will be teeming with them if left for long enough. But they're found in greater numbers (and grow especially quickly) inside beef, pork and chicken, which is why we usually cook meat and fish to kill off the bugs inside before we eat it. It is possible to eat raw meat if it's very, very fresh, but it doesn't take long before the bacteria begin to multiply and the meat 'goes bad'.

Smoking or salting (curing) meat and fish will help kill off the nasty bacteria too.

Okay – last question. How many different colours can sick go?

Lots. As I said, it mostly depends on what you've eaten. But there are a few colours that are serious danger signs when

Bile is a neon-yellow-green digestive liquid made in your liver and stored in your gall bladder, which helps to digest fats. See page 62 for more detail on what it does in the body.

they crop up. Bright yellow or green vomit often means you've emptied your stomach, and **bile** is flowing into it from the gall bladder and intestines below. It may not be such a bad sign in itself, but if you've puked that much, you may need to **rehydrate** with water and salts to recover fully.

More worrying is red, black or rusty-brown vomit. These can be signs of bleeding in the throat, oesophagus or stomach. So if you see these colours, you may want to see a doctor, sharpish.

What about bright blue or purple sick?

That just means you've been eating the crayons again. So stop it.

Oh. Oops!

If fatty foods make you fat, do sugary foods make you sweet?

Not really, no. In fact, it's sugary foods – not fatty ones – that make most people overweight. And while eating too much fat isn't healthy we do need some fat in our diets to keep our bodies in good condition.

Hold on – what? You mean I need to be fat to be healthy?

Not 'be fat', no. Being overweight can cause all sorts of other problems in your body. But if you want to stay healthy then you do need to *eat* fat. You need *all three* of the major food types – fat, protein and carbohydrates – to build and protect all the tissues of a strong, healthy body. It's just a case of getting the right stuff in the right amounts. In the end, you are – quite literally – what you eat.

Exactly. So if you EAT fat, you ARE fat, right?

Well, it's not quite as simple as that, I'm afraid.

Why?

Because, for starters, most foods contain at least two of the three food groups. Most vegetables, for example, contain both proteins and carbohydrates, while meat and fish contain protein, fat *and* carbohydrates. Plus, all these food types are processed in complex ways. When you swallow a lump of meaty protein, it isn't just sucked immediately into a muscle. It's digested, broken down, passed into your bloodstream and may be used as an energy source or building block within any one of your body's tissues. And the same goes for fats and carbohydrates.

How Different Food Types Are Used

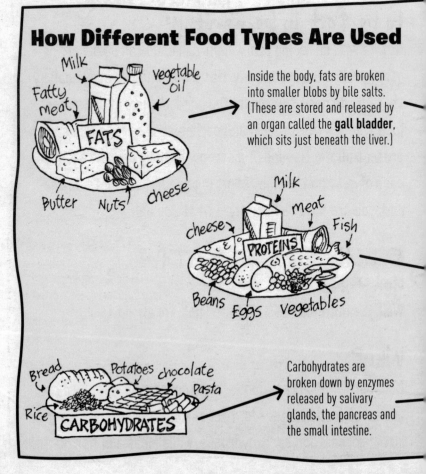

Milk
Vegetable Oil
Fatty meat
FATS
Butter Nuts cheese

Inside the body, fats are broken into smaller blobs by bile salts. (These are stored and released by an organ called the **gall bladder**, which sits just beneath the liver.)

Milk
Meat
cheese
PROTEINS
Fish
Beans Eggs Vegetables

Bread Potatoes chocolate
Pasta
Rice CARBOHYDRATES

Carbohydrates are broken down by enzymes released by salivary glands, the pancreas and the small intestine.

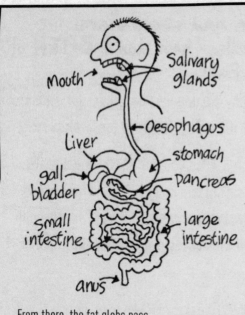

Mouth

Salivary glands

Oesophagus

Liver

stomach

gall bladder

pancreas

small intestine

large intestine

anus

An **enzyme** is a type of protein that breaks down or joins together other molecules. Enzymes in washing powder break down oily stains on your clothes. Enzymes in your body do all sorts of clever things, including breaking down food, building muscle tissue, destroying bacteria and copying DNA.

From there, the fat globs pass to the small intestine, where special enzymes called **lipases** break them down into small **fatty acids**.

These are then absorbed and either used for energy, used to build the membranes around cells or stored in fat (or **adipose**) cells.

Once inside the body, special enzymes called **proteases** – released by the stomach, pancreas and small intestine – break proteins down into **amino acids**.

These are then used for energy, to build new body tissues, to build antibodies for the immune system or for any number of other clever purposes in the body.

In the end, most of what's left is simple **glucose**. Once absorbed into the bloodstream, glucose is either used immediately for energy, used to build fibrous tissues, stored in muscles, or converted to fatty acids and stored in fat cells.

But if both fats and sugars are stored in fat cells, then don't BOTH of them make you fat?

In short, yes. But in reality it's usually the sugars (or, rather, the carbohydrates) that do it. This happens for two reasons:

1 Fat makes you feel full when you eat it, which generally prevents you from eating too much. That's why you can easily polish off a massive bowl of pasta, but getting through a similar-sized bowl filled with beefburgers would be much harder work.

2 Fat can be expensive. Steaks, chicken legs, pork chops, rich cheeses and exotic nuts are all very costly compared with bread, rice, white pasta and potatoes. Which is why most of us fill up on carbohydrates, with just a small portion of meat on top, on the side, or in between.

But that's a good thing, isn't it?

Yes, that's fine. As long as you eat the right kinds of carbohydrates, and not too much of the wrong ones.

CARBOHYDRATES

The Right Kind

Beans, vegetables, brown rice and brown bread

Make you feel fuller for longer because they contain complex carbohydrates which take a long time to digest.

The Wrong Kind

Sugar, sweets, chocolate, white rice, white bread and white pasta

Leave you feeling hungry again soon after eating them because they break down very quickly in the body. Because of this, you're more likely to eat too much of them, and more of the sugars released in digestion will be stored as fat.

Perhaps worst of all, too many sugary foods can mess up your body's ability to control the level of sugar in your blood meaning they also increase your risk of developing other problems like diabetes, high blood pressure and heart disease.

So what's the right amount to eat?

It depends on your age, your body type and the way your body processes food. But one good way of balancing your foods is to split your dinner plate into quarters (not literally — your mum won't thank you for that).

Then you fill the first quarter with foods rich in fat and protein, like meat, fish or beans. The second quarter, you load with carbohydrates like rice, pasta or potatoes. Then the remaining half, you fill with vegetables like green beans or salad greens. Stick to that, and you can't go too far wrong.

Wait a minute — where does the ice cream and chocolate come into all this?

After dinner, not instead of it. Eat a good, balanced diet, and you can happily enjoy a scoop of ice cream or a few chunks of chocolate each day.

Phew! That's a relief. Okay, so let's talk about these scoops ... Am I allowed to use a shovel?

[Sigh] I give up.

Get It Sorted – Rubbish Dump

Everything you eat and drink flows into your digestive system (namely, your stomach and guts). There, the whole lot mixes together into a messy sludge, and nutrients and water are drawn out into the bloodstream. The undigested stuff left in your digestive system then exits your body as faeces (i.e. poo). This is called excretion.

The other major way your body gets rid of wastes is through urine. This is made in your urinary system, by filtering excess water and wastes from your blood, and this happens in your kidneys.

Puzzle:
Diet and Digestion Wordsearch

Have you digested all these gut-related words? Find as many as you can in the grid below. (Double your score if you can remember what they all mean!) Answers on page 152.

amino acids   carbohydrates   fats   fatty acids
gall bladder   intestine   lipases   lipids
liver   oesophagus   peristalsis   proteases
proteins   starches   stomach   sugars

```
I S D Y P E R I S T A L S I S E C X S G C L
B U K H S T O X K V O V I N T E S T I N E C
F G A V I A V U R M E U N V S O Q Y R R W Q
M A C X Q G A L L B L A D D E R G Z K W Y E
P H J L P S V T Z R M P T S K R S A T X G L
H P P G A K T A L I P I D S T U E N I G O L
P O S I O G Y A N M X L F U I A S O D A H T
Y S G Z H N S O F P I F A T T Y A C I D S Z
Y E U W B C A R B O H Y D R A T E S N M A S
X O N G P C R V D M D G X P R O T E I N S Q
H G R L I P A S E S T O M A C H O W P S D S
U M R D X J U X K Z R J G D D P R K Y X Y T
H L S U G A R S E H C R A T S H P J F D R Q
L B E M U J I D N U D Z S N A W C J P S N T
```

Why do teeth fall out, and why don't they grow back in grown-ups?

Baby (or 'milk') teeth are temporary chompers that fall out to make room for bigger, stronger adult teeth later on. Adult teeth fall out when they become damaged, decayed and infected by bacteria. Once this second set of teeth has grown in, you're done. When they're gone, they're gone. This is because nature figures you're set for life, and the gene that controls regrowth of your gnashers switches off.

Hang on a mo – why do we even have milk teeth? Why don't we just grow one set and keep 'em?

Because the wide, strong set of teeth you need as an adult would be too big for your head (or rather, your jaw) as a baby. That said, you still need some kind of chompers to get you through your first years of life. So milk teeth (or, as dentists

69

call them, **deciduous teeth**) are tiny, temporary 'pegs' that do the job while your jawbones are still growing.

What job? It's not as if you need a full set of teeth to eat baby food. It's all mashed up already!

Ah, but that's because someone else has done the mashing already. In the modern, developed world, machines in baby-food factories mash up baby food during the production process. Elsewhere — and throughout history, before we had machines — parents would pre-mash or pre-chew solid food for their babies before giving it to them. But, either way, someone (or something) has to do the mashing.

Because, basically, that's what teeth are for. They mash up solid food into small, soft lumps that can be swallowed and digested without damaging — or getting stuck in — your digestive system.

As you may already know, you have three main types of teeth in your jaw — **incisors**, **canines** and **molars**.

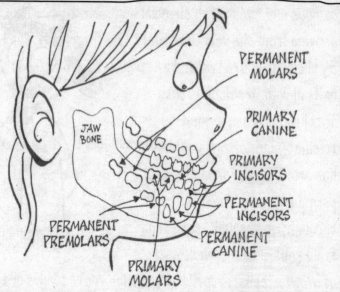

PERMANENT MOLARS

PRIMARY CANINE

PRIMARY INCISORS

PERMANENT INCISORS

PERMANENT CANINE

PRIMARY MOLARS

PERMANENT PREMOLARS

JAW BONE

Molars (and their smaller cousins, the premolars) are chewing teeth. They're used for grinding nuts and seeds, breaking up tough, chewy plant and animal tissues, and mashing each mouthful of food into a soft pulp.

Canines are grabbing and tearing teeth, used for ripping chunks of meat off the bone.

Incisors are blade-like shearing teeth, which help slice into your food.

So how many teeth do we have?

A normal adult human has thirty-two teeth — sixteen in the upper jaw and sixteen in the lower jaw.

To locate them all for yourself, see the **DIY Dentistry** *box on page 76.*

But they don't all grow through at once. For the first set of milk teeth, the incisors grow first, when you're between five and eight months old. Then come the

71

canines and molars (which start arriving from one year onwards). By the time you're two and a half, all your deciduous teeth are through. Then around six to eight years of age, your jaw has grown large enough for your permanent adult teeth to come through. So the milk teeth begin falling out, and the whole cycle

of growth repeats itself. By the time you're twelve or thirteen, all but your third set of molars (the wisdom teeth) will be present. (These may or may not come through later on, usually around eighteen to twenty-one years, but sometimes much later and sometimes not at all.)

There have been rare cases of elderly people growing lost adult teeth back, but these are very rare exceptions and you definitely shouldn't expect it to happen.

After that, you're done. Then it's just a case of looking after your permanent teeth for life — protecting them from damage, decay and disease. If one of these teeth gets knocked out by a hockey stick, or eaten down to the root by bacteria, then chances are it won't grow back again. Ever.

Warning!

But why not? Why can't damaged teeth repair themselves, or grow back again after they fall out?

As a matter of fact, your teeth *are* repairing themselves all the time. Just as bones grow continually (but slowly) and reshape themselves throughout life, so do your teeth. Teeth grow from the soft root and pulp below into the hard outer dentine and enamel layers above. As the surface of a tooth is worn down from use, it is slowly replaced by new tissue from within.

But if bacteria are allowed to grow on a tooth, and eat down through the enamel and dentine into the pulp and root, then the tooth can't repair itself quickly enough.

So the body seals off the root of the damaged tooth to protect itself from further infection. (A similar thing happens

if the tooth is deeply cracked or knocked out in an accident.) With no more blood supply, the tooth will rot and die. So it either falls out by itself, or (more often) it has to be extracted by a dentist.

This is why it's so important to **brush**, **floss** and **rinse** your teeth every day. This prevents the bacteria from building up and eating rapidly into your teeth. And since bacteria love feeding on sugar, it's especially important to clean your teeth after sugary snacks. Looked after properly, your teeth can last an entire lifetime. But more often diet, decay, damage and accidents mean that most people end up losing some or all of their teeth by the time they reach sixty or seventy.

So then you have to get false ones?

Usually, yes. Once you reach adulthood, the gene that controls the natural regrowth of lost teeth gets switched off, so any lost adult teeth must be replaced with artificial teeth made of a hard plastic. If you lose all your teeth, you may need dentures – which are basically a full set of upper and lower acrylic teeth, complete with moulded plastic gums that slip over your own. They're usually held in place by sticky gels or adhesives, to stop them dropping out into your dinner. **Urrgh!**

Yuck! I hope that never happens to me.

Well, it may never do so. Recently, scientists have been working on ultrasound implants that help stimulate teeth to repair themselves, and on special gene-therapy gels that may one day allow you to regrow lost teeth altogether!

Cool!

But . . . they're not quite ready to roll yet, and even when they are, they will probably be very expensive. So the smart thing to do is . . .

I know, I know – look after the chompers you've already got.

Exactly. So if you want to dodge the dentures, you'd better keep brushing!

Experiment: DIY Dentistry!

Adult humans have thirty-two permanent teeth. Depending on your age, you may or may not have them all just now – some might not have grown through yet, and may be temporarily missing. But see how many you can find. Grab a hand mirror, open wide and follow these instructions to ID your teeth, just like your dentist does!

1 First, the incisors. These are the two flat, horsey-looking teeth at the front, along with the two smaller teeth on either side. You should have eight altogether – four upper incisors, and four lower incisors.

2 Behind those are the more pointy-looking canines. These may be quite pointy, or rounded at the bottom. Either way, they usually stick out a little compared to the teeth in front and behind. You should have a total of four canines – two upper, two lower.

3 Behind those are the flatter, squarer premolars. You should have eight of these – two on each side of the mouth, behind the canines, in both the upper and lower jaw.

4 Finally, we come to the molars. These are large, square, flat-bottomed teeth right at the back. By your teens, there should be at least two on each side of the mouth in both the upper and lower jaw, giving a total of eight molars. After that, most (but not all) people grow a third set of four molars – known as wisdom teeth – that sit behind the original eight.

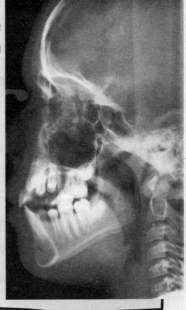

Eight incisors + **four** canines + **eight** premolars + **twelve** molars = **thirty-two** teeth altogether. How many did you find?

Why does your tummy rumble when you're hungry?

Because when your brain senses that you're hungry it empties your stomach, squeezing out stomach gases and half-digested slop to make room for the lovely grub to come. As these gases and liquids gurgle through your guts, they create loud rumbling noises in your belly.

Really? Like gurgling drainpipes inside your body?

Exactly. Only the pipes are meaty, and have more twists and turns. And they're filled with half-digested, liquid food (or **chyme**) rather than rainwater.

Hmmm. It doesn't sound much like a gurgle in my belly. More like a growling bear or something.

That's because the sound changes as it vibrates through the muscle, meaty fibres and skin of your belly, so that by the time it gets to the outside, the sound is much lower-pitched. Technically, tummy rumbles are called **borborgymi**. And you're right — by the time they get to the outside, they sound more like low

And if you say 'borborgymi' in a silly, low-pitched voice, it sounds like just like the thing it describes!

Make sure you ask permission – or at least warn the person – before you do this. Otherwise you'll get some very strange looks.

growls than tinkly gurgles. But, if you put your ear to someone's belly just as it rumbles, you'll hear the high gurgly bit beneath the rumble, which you can't normally hear from a distance.

But why would you want your stomach to squeeze shut if you're about to eat something? Wouldn't you want it to stay open, so you can digest things?

It doesn't really squeeze shut, it just contracts a bit to push out the stuff that's still in there, in order to make room for more. And, in fact, not much digestion goes on in the stomach at all.

Eh? I thought the stomach had acids in it that melt and digest your food for you ...

Well, it does contain acids that break the food down a bit. And, together with the churning, mashing muscles of the stomach wall, these help liquefy your food. This is partly to make digestion easier later on, but mostly so you can fit more grub in your stomach at once. The main function of the stomach is to receive mashed-up food blobs from the mouth and hold them in storage for a bit, before they're passed through the gut for digestion.

Okay . . . so how does your brain know you're hungry in the first place?

Basically, it senses changes in the levels of sugars and fats in your bloodstream. When levels drop too low, the brain releases clever chemical messengers (called **hormones**) into your blood that make you feel hungry, and want to seek out food. Then when you finally find food it sends quicker signals (through nerves) to your mouth, stomach and gut, preparing them for fast and efficient grub intake. Often, even *looking* at food can be enough to trigger these nerve signals.

Is that why we sometimes drool and slobber when we see tasty-looking foods?

Yep – spot on. When you haven't eaten for a while, and you're suddenly presented with a steak, cake or milkshake, you'll start to drool from salivary glands under your tongue and at the back of your mouth. As you munch and chew, the saliva starts to break down starchy bits of your food, and keeps it moist so that it slides down your food tube (or oesophagus) more easily.

Russian biologist and psychologist Ivan Pavlov discovered these brain-body (or psychosomatic) signals. He revealed them by ringing a bell every time he fed a group of dogs. After a while, the dogs would drool at the sound of the bell alone, proving that it wasn't the food itself that was making the dogs slobber – it was the thought of food (or, rather, hearing something that made them think of food, even if the food wasn't present).

A Brain-Body Experiment:

1 Imagine you're lost in a hot, dry desert, and you haven't eaten for days.

2 Now picture in your mind, a huge, fat, juicy hamburger. Really see it in your mind's eye, every detail – the rich, juicy meat . . . the crunchy lettuce beneath . . . the wet, juicy tomato on top . . .

3 Now imagine raising the burger to your open mouth . . . the smell of it wafting up your nostrils as you take a big, juicy bite . . .

4 Drooling yet?

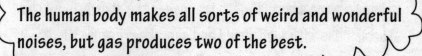

The human body makes all sorts of weird and wonderful noises, but gas produces two of the best.

Farts

Farts contain oxygen and nitrogen from the air that you swallow with your food, carbon dioxide from swallowed air, fizzy drinks and fizzing stomach acids, and more carbon dioxide – plus hydrogen, hydrogen sulphide and methane – produced by bacteria in the lower intestine. That's a lot of gas!

The average healthy person creates a daily 1–2.5 litres (2–4 pints) of gas, and releases it – in the shape of individual farts – about twelve to sixteen times a day.

Baked beans *really do* make you fart. They contain a sugar called stachoise which is hard for human guts to break down. So bacteria try to do it for us, producing a lot of gas in the process. So beans really are the 'musical fruit'. (The more you eat, the more you toot . . .)

Burps

If you swallow air while you eat or drink (or on purpose if you're trying to force a burp) it gets trapped in the stomach. As the stomach fills with food, liquid and gas, the pressure builds up and the air bursts through a flap called the **cardia** (which closes off the stomach from the food-tube, or **oesophagus**), and... BRRRRRRRRRPPPPPPP!

Of course if you want to force the burp out, you can squeeze your stomach by contracting your stomach muscles and **diaphragm** (which is the flat sheet of muscle underneath your stomach and lungs). Drinking lots of fizzy drinks helps too as they're made bubbly and fizzy by adding carbon dioxide under pressure. So when you drink the drink, you swallow the gas. The gas builds up in your stomach and...

ALL SKIN AND BONES

If you can break a bone, could you snap a muscle?

Yes, you can. But this rarely happens as it's very difficult to do, because special sensors inside stop you from snapping, ripping or tearing your muscles on purpose. In any case, if you do break a bone or tear a muscle, the injury will usually heal up all by itself.

Don't be silly. Bones don't repair themselves.

Yes, they do.

They don't.

All right, then — how do you think broken bones get repaired?

Well, **doctors** do it, don't they. With X-rays and plaster casts and stuff.

Ah, but it's not the doctors, X-rays or plaster casts that *do* the healing. X-rays allow doctors to look inside the body and see which bones (if any) are broken. If there *is* a break, then the doctor simply nudges the bone back into place, and the bone begins to repair itself. New bone tissue grows to seal the split

If it's a **really** bad break, doctors or surgeons sometimes have to insert metal pins or screws into the bones to hold them in place while they heal. But most of the time this isn't necessary, and all they have to do is push the bone back into place and hold it there while the nurse wraps the area in bandages and plaster.

(or **fracture**) within weeks, without any help from doctors, nurses or anyone else.

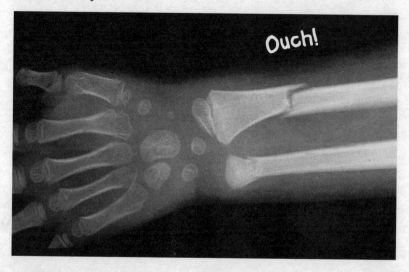

Ouch!

Top 10 commonly broken bones

1) Wrist
2) Clavicle (or collarbone)
3) Hip
4) Finger
5) Toe
6) Foot
7) Ankle
8) Arm
9) Nose
10) Jaw

Not in perfect order, since not all broken fingers and toes are reported or treated in hospital, and different age groups tend to break different bones. In people over seventy-five, the hip is the most common break. In young children it's the collarbone, and so on.

So what's the plaster cast for, then?

The plaster cast simply holds the bones still so that they can carry out their amazing self-repair job undisturbed. In fact, in some parts of Asia, doctors don't even apply plaster casts to broken bones. They just align the bones, tell the patient not to use the broken limb, and send 'em home. After that, they simply check in every week or so to make sure the bones are healing straight.

Seriously? That actually works?

As long as the break isn't too serious (like a completely shattered bone, or a **compound fracture** that pushes a snapped bit of bone through the skin), then yes – absolutely. Left alone to

EEEEEWWWW!

do its job, a broken bone will happily heal itself. Your bones, you see, are constantly regrowing and reshaping themselves throughout your lifetime. Special bone-building cells called **osteoblasts** are creating new bone tissue all the time, regrowing the bone from the inside out. Meanwhile, special bone-eating cells called **osteoclasts** are constantly munching away at your bone tissue — removing old, dead bone cells and maintaining the shape of the bone by chiselling away at the edges like tiny microscopic sculptors.

These bone-builders and bone-eaters remodel your bones throughout your entire lifetime. In fact, within seven years, every bone cell in your body has been regrown and replaced. So if you're over seven years old, you have a completely different skeleton from the one you were born with. And if you're over fourteen, you've regrown your entire skeleton twice!

Top 10 bone-breaking sports

Again, not in perfect order, but you get the idea!

1) Base jumping
2) Rock climbing
3) Motorcycle racing
4) Bull riding
5) Horse riding
6) Heli-skiing
7) Rugby
8) Soccer
9) Skateboarding
10) Roller-skating

No way!

Yes, way. So, you see, your bones are repairing themselves all the time. Breaking a bone simply kicks this process into emergency overdrive.

Here's how it works:

Let's say you forget to wear your shin pads to football practice, and a nasty tackle breaks your fibula.

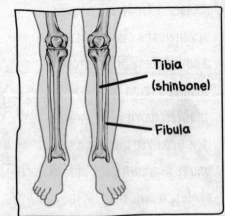

Tibia (shinbone)

Fibula

The bone has snapped in the middle, but the two halves are still held more or less in place by the muscles and fibrous tissues all around them. The bone itself is a hollow tube, with hard bone tissue on the outside and fleshier **bone marrow** on the inside. Right away — before you've even been stretchered off the pitch — severed blood vessels within the marrow start to form a fleshy clot.

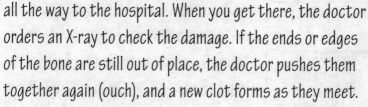

Provided that the split ends of your bones aren't too widely separated, this sticky blob will hold them in place all the way to the hospital. When you get there, the doctor orders an X-ray to check the damage. If the ends or edges of the bone are still out of place, the doctor pushes them together again (ouch), and a new clot forms as they meet. Otherwise, the doctor or nurse will simply hold the bones in place (by pressing on the sides of your leg) while they wrap the leg in bandages soaked in gooey liquid plaster. When the plaster hardens into a cast, it will hold the bones in place for several weeks or months while the healing continues.

Many hospitals now create casts using fibreglass bandages or special, heat-sensitive plastics instead. Depends where you go.

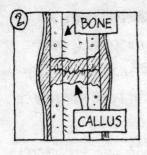

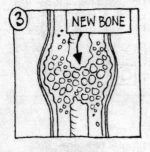

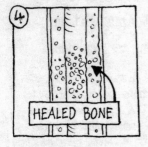

So then what happens?

After a week or so, special bone-marrow cells called **chondroblasts** replace the gooey clot holding the bone ends together with tough **collagen** fibres. This forms a knobbly, **fibrous callus**. This is tougher than the sticky clot, but still not strong enough to bear weight. Over the following weeks and months, osteoblasts (bone-builders) move into the callus and start to replace the collagen fibres with new bone tissue. On an X-ray, the break now looks like one bone with a big ball or bulge in the middle. Finally, osteoclasts (bone-eaters) chew away at the edges of the bulge until the bone looks like one thin, straight shin bone again. Within two to three months the bone will be fully healed, and you can start walking on it once more (although it might be a while longer before you can run and play football, since the muscles waste away inside the casts and need strengthening before you're back to your full abilities).

That's cool. It's like superhero super-healing or something. So do ripped muscles heal the same way?

Torn muscles are a little simpler, although they can take just as long to heal as broken bones and may need extra help to get back into shape. It's rare that a whole muscle will be torn, as there are little sensory organs within each one – called Golgi organs – that prevent you from stretching them to breaking point.

See 'What do double-jointed people look like on X-rays?' *on page 93 for more about tendons.*

It's usually the thinner tendons at the ends that tear first. But if the muscle is pulled very powerfully and suddenly while tense (this sometimes happens as a defender's boot clashes with the swinging thigh of a striker in football), the belly of the muscle can rip, causing a very painful injury. **YOWCH!**

Right away, the muscle forms a clot at the torn edges, and within a week collagen fibres grow to knit the ends together with tough scar tissue – in a similar way that the fibrous callus forms in bone. This 'heals' the muscle, but leaves it tight, inflexible and likely to rip again in other places. After that, it takes many months of exercise and physiotherapy for the scar tissue to be replaced with new, flexible muscle fibres.

Eventually, though, this will happen, and you can jog back on to the pitch once more.

So, if I hurt my leg or ankle playing football, how do I know if it's a broken bone or a ripped muscle?

Like I said, ripped and torn muscles are rare. If you do twist your ankle or leg on the pitch, the chances are you've just strained or sprained a muscle or tendon. (This is when the muscle or tendon gets overstretched, but doesn't actually tear or snap). A good quick check is to push *gently* on the end of an injured limb – whether it's a toe, ankle, leg, finger, wrist or arm – just hold it straight and press very gently in towards your body. If it's just strained, it'll be sore but not unbearable. If it's broken, it'll feel like someone just set fire to it, and it's off to the hospital for you.

Yeah, but then I'd get a cool plaster cast, and all my mates could sign it.

That's true. But, believe me, it's not worth it. Just wear your shin pads.

What do double-jointed people look like on X-rays?

They look about the same as everybody else. 'Double joints' don't show up on X-rays, because in reality there's no such thing. With a few very rare exceptions, we all have the same number of bones and joints. It's just that the tendons, ligaments and cartilage that tie the joints together behave a little differently in so called 'double-jointed' people.

What do you mean, there's no such thing as double joints?

It's true. Apart from a very few people (and we're talking one in a million here) with rare bone deformities, everyone has more or less the same number of bones and joints. So for the most part there's really no such thing as a 'double joint'.

Course there is. My mate Dave can bend his thumb all the way back to his forearm. And there's this girl in my PE class who can turn her elbows inside out AND put both feet behind her head. You're telling me they're not double-jointed?

Well, you can *call* those people 'double-jointed', but that doesn't mean they actually have double joints. The reason why these unusually flexible friends can bend and twist the way they do is not really to do with the shape of their bones. It's to do with the unusual length and stretchiness of their **ligaments**, **tendons** and **cartilage**.

What are they, then?
Ligaments are the tight little fleshy cords that tie the ends of bones together.

If you have a model skeleton in your school's science or biology lab, you may have noticed that there are little metal wires holding the bones together. Without them, the whole thing would fall apart. Well, ligaments basically go where these wires are — between the bones in your skeleton.

How many bones are there in your body?

It depends how old you are. You're born with 300–350 bones, but as you grow from baby into toddler many of these fuse together. By the time you're fully grown, you end up with a total of 206 solid bones in your body. These 206 bones are then tied together with around 900 ligaments.

So there's more than one ligament per bone?

Well spotted — yes. There are more than four times as many ligaments as bones, and most joints have more than one ligament holding them together. The shoulder joint, for example, contains three major bones — the **humerus** (or upper arm bone), the **scapula** (or shoulder blade) and the **clavicle** (or collarbone).

These three bones are held together by five major ligaments, plus a large number of tendons, muscles and bands of fibrous tissue. Ligaments stabilize joints by preventing the bones from separating too much. Unlike muscles, they're not very flexible. (Although they do stretch a little, you should think of them more like taut cables than bendy rubber bands).

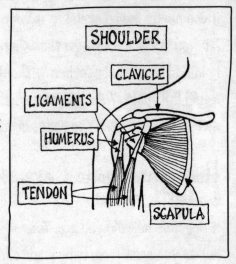

Next up are the **tendons**. Like ligaments, tendons are bands of fleshy tissue that tie bones together. But they also attach muscles to bones, and they're generally a bit more stretchy than ligaments, allowing more 'give' in the joint. Tendons far outnumber ligaments in the body — there are about 4,000 of them altogether — and while each joint usually only has one or two ligaments, there are usually several tendons overlapping each other, all around the joint.

The ends of bones are covered with a thin layer of tough, plastic-like material called **cartilage**. Cartilage helps to lubricate the joints, stopping the bones from grinding against one another too much, and also helps absorb impacts along the length of the joint. If the cartilage gets torn or damaged (footballers often have this injury in their knee joints), it can be very painful, and it prevents the joint from moving freely.

So do double-jointed people have extra-long ligaments or super-stretchy tendons or something?

That's pretty much it, yes. So-called 'double-jointed' people may have **u n u s u a l l y l o n g   l i g a m e n t s** that, for example, allow them to bend their fingers or thumbs back on themselves without snapping. Or they may have

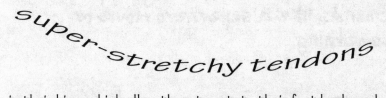

in their hips, which allow them to rotate their feet backwards, or place their ankles behind their heads. And your friend with the freaky backwards elbows probably has unusually long or stretchy ligaments and tendons in her shoulder joints, which allow her to pop the humerus right out of the socket and back again. Most 'double-jointed' people also have more pliable cartilage between their joints, which can be stretched or twisted further before ripping and tearing.

So why can't you see these things on X-rays?

Because X-rays only reveal bones inside the body. Tendons, ligaments and cartilage aren't dense enough to absorb X-rays, which go straight through, leaving dark, empty patches on the X-ray plate. So unless the 'double-jointed' person shows some other sign of his/her stretchy tendons – such as an unusually wide gap between the bones of the hip or shoulder – then their secret ability will be invisible to their doctors.

Coooool. Secret stretchy people. Sounds like a superhero movie or something.

So could I develop super-bendy joints by stretching my tendons or taking my cartilage out?

You can't do it all at once, no. Overstretching your tendons all at once or removing your cartilage would lead to *less* flexibility in the joints, not more (not to mention a lot of pain). But you *can* stretch tendons over time with some types of exercise like yoga. It may take months or years of practice to get super-bendy, and your tendons may never be as bendy as someone with naturally loose and flexible tendons and ligaments. But if you stick at it, you too could be impressing your friends with your freaky fingers and bendy legs. Try the exercise below to get started.

Wicked. Sign me up!

Bendy Arms

Kneel down on the floor and place your palms on the ground in front of your knees. Now keep your palms on the ground, but rotate your hands outwards until your fingers and thumbs are pointing back towards you. Inhale, then exhale as you sit back on your heels, leaving your hands in place. Your elbows should be straight and your palms pressed into the ground. Hold for thirty seconds. This will stretch and strengthen your wrists, elbows and forearms.

How do karate masters chop through concrete?

They simply drive the tough bones of their hands through the slab or block at high speed, aiming at just the right spot. Though you may not believe it, bones are actually much tougher than concrete. So, if it's done right, the karate-chop battle of bone-versus-block only has one winner.

Bones are tougher than concrete? No way! That's impossible!

It's true. Living bone is a far stronger material than artificial concrete. In fact, if you used a machine to snap a human leg bone, then did the same thing with a concrete cylinder of the same basic shape and weight, the leg bone could withstand over *forty times* more force before snapping. **Whoa!**

So if my bones were made of concrete, they would break more easily?

Exactly.

But how? I thought concrete was some of the toughest stuff around. Isn't that why we build buildings and bridges out of it?

rete certainly is a very tough material. But it's also

quite brittle, and cracks easily if bent or twisted. Try to bend, twist or crush a piece of bone and it will bend quite a bit before it cracks, and this is where bone has the advantage. From the outside, bone seems like a dry, brittle material. But in fact it's more like a very thick, solid gel, with chalky

Solid concrete sections of bridges and buildings are reinforced with steel rods. If they weren't, they could easily be damaged or destroyed by high winds or earth tremors.

minerals trapped inside. Cut a living bone open, and you'll see that the bit in the middle — the marrow — is spongy and fleshy. (This is missing from most dinosaur bones in museums, as it has long since rotted away or fossilized.)

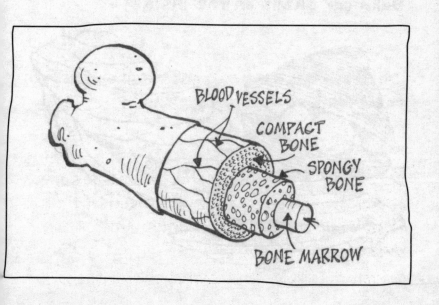

BLOOD VESSELS

COMPACT BONE

SPONGY BONE

BONE MARROW

If you want to see for yourself just how bendy bones can be, try the experiment on page 106.

As the bone grows, living bone cells from the marrow, called **osteocytes**, surround themselves with a criss-crossing web of protein and sugar molecules. This fleshy, fibrous web then traps water, along with calcium and phosphorus, squeezed into it by the osteocytes. Over time, the web hardens into a chalky gel, rich in calcium phosphate — the same material that clams, oysters and mussels use to build their shells.

So we're a bit like shellfish, only we build our shells on the inside?

You could say that, yes. Anyway, what you end up with is a very tough, strong material which is also very lightweight. Better still, because of its partly fleshy, watery structure, bone isn't brittle like concrete. In many ways, it's the ideal building material. If we could build houses and bridges out of it, we probably would. (Who knows — someday, maybe we will!)

Is that why a bony hand can chop through a concrete block?

Partly, yes. The bones in your hand are many times stronger than wooden boards, clay tiles, or even concrete blocks. Plus your hand-bones are reinforced with a covering of muscles, tendons, cartilage and skin. As a solid lump of flesh, your hand could easily slap through a concrete block if you hit it hard enough.

So could I chop a block in half like a karate master?

In theory, yes. Anyone with healthy bones could do it. But without the proper training I wouldn't try it.

Why's that?

Because karate masters take no chances.

Step-By-Step Karate

1 Karate masters spend months or years toughening up the skin of their hands by hitting wooden posts wrapped in string, or boards covered in foam.

2 Karate masters practise hitting the boards, blocks or tiles with enough speed. (They also practise with thin wooden boards before having a crack at concrete or tiles.)

3 Karate masters practise hitting the block with just the right point of the hand, like the first two knuckles of the fist or the blade-like edge of the hand.

4 Karate masters practise hitting the block in just the right place. They aim right for the centre of the board, tile or block.

What if I took some tiles out of my dad's shed and had a go at it right now? What would happen then?

You'd probably break a finger or cut your hand. And all your friends would laugh.

Oh. I guess I shouldn't try that, then.

No. You shouldn't. Trust me, there are easier – and far less painful – ways to impress your mates.

Experiment: Bendy Bones

As hard and chalky as they seem, it's hard to imagine that our bones are actually quite flexible, and made mostly of water. If you want to see for yourself, just try this experiment with a chicken bone from the butcher's . . .

1 Get a leftover wing bone or wishbone from the butcher, and ask him (or a helpful parent) to clean off all the flesh, muscles and tendons. Then leave it overnight to dry. (Be sure to hide it from your cat or dog, or they'll make off with it and ruin the progress of science!)

2 Try bending it between your fingers. It probably won't bend much, but have a go. Don't break it, though!

3 Grab a bottle of vinegar, and a glass jar with a tight-fitting lid. Put the bone in the jar, and fill it with enough vinegar to cover it completely.

4 Screw the lid on, and leave it alone for one full week.

5 Unscrew the jar, pour out the vinegar, remove the bone, and rinse it with water.

6 Try bending the bone between your fingers, as you did before. What happens?

(See page 152 for the answer, and why this works.)

Why do we have toes?

The simple answer is we inherited our toes from our tree-dwelling animal ancestors, who used them to climb, dangle and swing on branches. Later on, as two-legged humans, we kept them because they proved useful for walking, running and leaping.

You mean we inherited them from monkeys?

Not quite. We didn't actually evolve from monkeys. But our ape-like ancestors did have gripping (or prehensile) feet, which they used to grip tree branches just as modern-day monkeys do.

And, in fact, we can trace our toes a lot further back than that. Long before our animal ancestors evolved into apes, they were little shrew-like mammals with four paws and five toes on each. Before that, they were four-legged, five-toed reptiles. And, before *that*, four-legged amphibians, much like big newts.

So ALL animals have five toes on each foot?

With a few exceptions, yes. Fish, of course, never had toes in the first place. And invertebrates (animals without backbones) like insects, crabs and squid have very different body structures to vertebrates (or animals with backbones). So they don't count here.

Among the vertebrates, some animals (like snakes and whales) had feet and toes once, but have since lost them altogether, while others (like horses) stand on enlarged middle toes (the other toes shrivelled up and reduced beside them). But the vast majority of mammals, birds, reptiles and amphibians have five toes on each foot. So, like them, we have five toes.

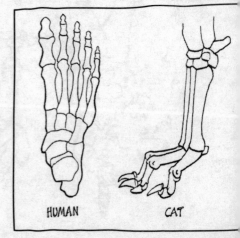

HUMAN   CAT

But why FIVE toes, and not three, six or nine?

That's a good question. No one knows for sure. We do know that the first animals with feet — prehistoric amphibians that emerged from the oceans around 400 million years ago — actually had seven or eight toes on each foot. But within a few million years five-toed land animals started to become more common, and seven-and eight-toed animals began to die off. For some reason, five turned out to be the ideal number of feety digits. And since most of today's vertebrate land animals (including us) evolved from those five-toed pioneers, most of them (or, rather, *us*) have five toes too.

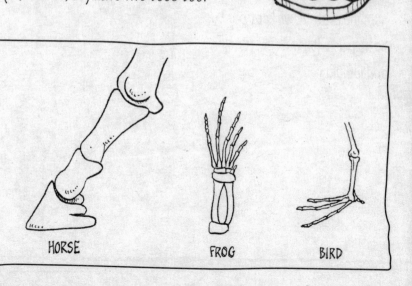

HORSE   FROG   BIRD

Okay, so I understand how bendy, finger-like toes would've come in handy for tree-swinging monkey-and-lemur-type things. But what good did they do us once we came down from the trees?

When our ape-like ancestors left the safety of the trees and started walking upright on the plains and savannahs of Africa, their toes got shorter and stubbier over time, so that they were no longer much use for climbing. But, as it turned out, stubby toes were still quite handy for balancing upright on two feet. So, as early and modern humans evolved, we kept our toes to help us with walking, running and jumping.

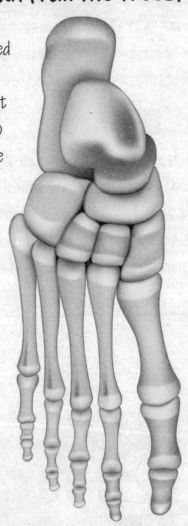

Experiment: Toes Really Do Make a Difference

1 Take your shoes off, and stand upright on a flat surface.
Now lift one foot, and balance on the other for a minute or more.
What happens?

2 Now do it again, but this time lift all the toes on your supporting foot off the ground. What happens now?

3 Now go back to the first experiment, and try to feel what your toes are doing. Feel the tension in the muscles of your toes come and go as you wobble to and fro.

While you may not always notice it, your toes are constantly making tiny adjustments (called **micro-adjustments**) to your balance while you're standing. These little pushes from your toes keep your centre of balance (in this case, your hips) above your feet, stopping you from toppling forward or backwards. As you stand, your big toes alone bear around a quarter of your total weight.

4 Now try walking or running with your toes pulled up to see what it might be like without toes – you'll probably look more like a clumsy chicken than an Olympic athlete!

Okay, so if toes are so great, how come it hurts so much when you stub one on a chair?

YAAAAH!?

Because your toes need lots of sensory nerves in order to sense the shape and slope of the ground beneath them. This allows you to walk over almost any terrain without constantly looking down. But, unfortunately, alongside these touch-sensitive toe-nerves is another set of nerves that sense pain. *These* are there to stop you whacking your toes into things too hard, and damaging the delicate sensory nerves and tissues inside. So when you stub your toe on something they really let you know it! Best thing you can do is rub and squeeze, to help soften the pain with more touch.

That totally sucks, dude.

Toe-tally?

Oh, very funny.

Why do your fingers go wrinkly in the bath?

Because your skin is actually an organ system made up of separate layers of tissue. Spend too long in the bath, and the dry outer layer will expand and spread out while the layer beneath stays put. This creates folds and wrinkles in spots where your skin is especially tight — like your feet, hands and fingertips. Some scientists think that the wrinkles may help us get a grip on wet, slippery objects.

Wait – skin is an organ?

Yes, it is. In fact, it's the largest organ in the body.

But I thought organs were, y'know, like big lumps of meaty stuff . . .

Well, an organ is just a collection of tissues that work together for a common purpose. And while most organs are a bit easier to play football with, that doesn't mean your skin doesn't qualify.

Skin isn't just a flat, boring sheet of body tissue. It's actually very complex. It's made up of two separate tissue layers — called the **dermis** and **epidermis** — and also contains other tissues like hair, nails, glands and nerve endings.

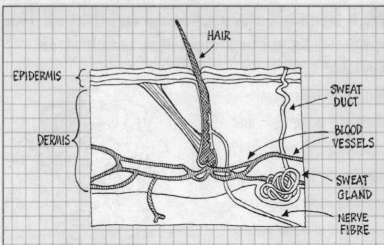

EPIDERMIS

HAIR

DERMIS

SWEAT DUCT

BLOOD VESSELS

SWEAT GLAND

NERVE FIBRE

Get It Sorted – Skin

The DERMIS (which is just Latin for 'skin') is a rich, living layer of skin cells, blood vessels, sweat glands and oil glands. This is the pink, bloody bit that gets exposed if you manage to graze or chop off more than a few millimetres of skin in an accident. But ordinarily you never see it because above (or outside) this lies the epidermis.

The EPIDERMIS (which means 'outer skin') itself contains two layers – an outer layer of hard, dry, dead skin cells that are constantly shed from the body, and an underlying layer of living skin cells that grow, divide and push upwards to replace the ones you've shed. It's the *outer* part of the epidermis that goes wrinkly in the bath. This is because the cells in the under-layer are firmly attached to each other and to the dermis beneath. But the cells in the outer layer are not. So when your warm bath water is absorbed into the dry, outer layer of the epidermis, it swells up, spreads out, and forms ripples and wrinkles.

Why doesn't your skin go wrinkly all the time – like every time you wash your hands?

Because ordinarily your epidermis is kept oily and waterproof by oil glands in the dermis. But if you spend too long underwater (and especially in warm water) the oil gets washed out and water begins to seep in. The longer you stay in the bath,  the more water is absorbed and the wrinklier you get.

So if you stayed in there long enough, would you end up looking like an old granny? Or a big raisin?

Thankfully, no. There's only so much water your skin can absorb, so there's a limit to how wrinkly you get.

That's a relief. So is that what skin is for, then? To keep water out?

Actually, it's designed to keep water in, rather than out. Since your body is 60–75 per cent water, it has to keep as much of it in as possible, only allowing out small amounts through sweat, tears and urine. So the tough, oily barrier of your skin helps prevent your body from dehydrating. And, as an organ system, skin does loads of other useful jobs within the body.

Multi-tasking Skin

- It's a barrier to water.
- It forms a fleshy shield against bacteria, viruses and other nasty microbes.
- It protects our bodies from harmful chemicals and radiation.
- It stores fat and water, which help to insulate the body against extreme temperatures.
- It helps to control our inner body temperature, using hairs and sweat glands to trap and release heat.
- It's a huge sense organ. Nerve endings embedded in your skin sense temperature, pressure and pain, and work together to give you your sense of touch.
- It helps with digestion and nutrition. Your skin uses sunlight to produce vitamin D, which helps you to absorb nutrients.
- It helps you get rid of things too. While body wastes and toxic chemicals are mostly peed and pooed out of your body, they're also sweated out through your skin.
- It can even absorb some vitamins and medicines that help to keep you healthy.

Tests have revealed that water-wrinkles help monkeys and humans pick up wet, slippery underwater objects. So finger-wrinkles may have evolved to help us pluck shellfish from rivers, ponds and shallow-surf waters. And toe-wrinkles may help us grip better when wading!

But you can't actually **eat** through your skin, right?

Right. Sadly, most food particles are too large to get through. And, even if you could absorb food through your skin, your immune cells would probably just attack the undigested food blobs once they made it into your bloodstream, thinking they were dangerous bacteria. So, while slapping on the beef stew like suntan lotion might be fun, it won't do you much good.

It may, however, make you very popular with your dog . . .

GREY MATTERS

Why does it feel weird when you step on to a stationary escalator?

Because your brain stores memories of how to keep your balance on a moving escalator, and goes on to 'escalator autopilot' just as you're about to step on. When it discovers the steps aren't moving, it takes a while for the autopilot to switch off, leaving you very surprised and confused!

My brain has an autopilot?

Sort of, yes.

Sweet! So can I switch it on in the mornings, and it'll get me out of

bed and off to school while I just chill out? I guess I could wake up and take over my body around 10, maybe . . .

Hang on, that's not . . .

... On second thoughts, why stop there? Why not just leave the autopilot on for the boring classes, and only take over for the fun ones, like Art and PE ...

Wait, wait! Hold up there. It doesn't work like that, I'm afraid.

It doesn't? Booo. Not fair. So you were just winding me up?

No, I wasn't. The brain really does have a kind of 'autopilot' function, which can take over your movements and help you do things you've done before without concentrating too much. But that doesn't mean you can 'check out' entirely ...

If you think about it, your brain has to have an 'autopilot', otherwise you'd have to learn complex movements — like riding a bike — over and over again. Or, at the very least, you'd have to concentrate so hard on staying on the bike that it'd be almost impossible to do anything else at the same time — like chat with friends, or listen to an MP3 player.

Hmmm. Never thought of that. So how DOES it work, then?

When you start to learn a new, complex movement skill — like walking, running or riding a bike — for a while you have to concentrate hard as you learn to balance your shifting weight and coordinate the movements of your arms and legs.

The movements are made using the brain's **motor cortex** — tiny parts of which control every individual bit of the body. But the *order* or *sequence* of walking, running or riding movements is controlled by a region at the back of the brain, called the **cerebellum**.

MOTOR CORTEX

CEREBELLUM

...ally, after many hours of practice, the whole shape and ...nce of each activity becomes permanently embedded in the cerebellum, as a kind of 'muscle memory'. After that, as soon as you start stepping, running or pedalling, the 'autopilot' function in your cerebellum kicks in, and you just *do* *it*, without thinking. Ever heard the expression '**It's just like riding a bike – you never forget**'? Well – that's why.

But what does that have to do with riding escalators? I mean, that's not exactly a SKILL, is it? You just step on and stand there.

Ah, but that's where you're wrong. Riding escalators *is* a skill – not a very impressive one, I admit, but still a skill. If you don't believe me, next time you head out to a multi-storey shopping centre or mall, take a seat near the escalator and wait for a toddler to come along. Then watch as the child tries to step on to it, leans back and almost falls over.

Don't worry – usually they're saved from falling by a parent tugging upwards on an outstretched hand.

The only reason *you* don't do this is because you've learned the skill of escalator-riding, and your autopilot takes over. Just as you learned to balance yourself automatically on a bike, you learned a little about how to mount, ride and dismount escalators the first few times you did it.

How to Ride an Escalator

1 **Lean forward** and **speed up** your walking pace as you get on.

2 Keep **leaning forward** a little (or grab the moving handrail) to compensate for the forward motion and avoid toppling back down the steps.

3 Take a **long, striding step off** the thing to avoid tripping up at the end of it.

Why does the handrail never move at quite the same speed as the steps on escalators? That's a question for the engineers, I suppose ...

Now, of course, all these movements are so automatic that you hardly have to think about them. That's because — like bike-riding — escalator-riding is stored permanently in your cerebellum. So, every time you approach an escalator, the autopilot kicks in and your brain starts to adjust your body to the steps automatically. Unfortunately, this still happens even when the escalator is broken, turning it — effectively — into *stairs*.

So then what happens?

Exactly what you'd expect. The brain preps your body for *moving* steps, making you lean forward and speed up your stride. But since the steps aren't actually moving this makes it feel as if you're being 'sucked into' the escalator.

This may be the root of the common fear that, if you don't get off in time, you'll be sucked down the hole at the end along with the moving steps. Ever felt that way?

But can't it TELL the steps aren't moving? I thought the brain was supposed to be clever . . .

Eventually, yes — the brain *can* tell. In fact, if you ride the same broken escalator twice, it most likely won't happen the second time, as your brain has figured it out. But the first time you approach a broken escalator, even though you can see it's not moving — the memory of '**HOW TO RIDE AN ESCALATOR**' is so strong that it overrides your conscious knowledge that you are, in fact,

approaching a flight of stairs. The effect is strongest when you walk straight off a working escalator and on to a broken (and stationary) one. Try it – it'll seriously freak you out.

I will. But I think I'll get my friends to do it first.

Motor Memory Weirdness

Broken escalators aren't the only things out there that generate weird movement sensations. Ever felt weird on one of these?

Moving walkways at airports

Similar to escalators. You learn to get on, ride them and get off on autopilot. But when they're out of order, if feels like you're sucked on to them and then wading through mud.

Ships and boats

After a good stretch of time bobbing around at sea, your brain adjusts your balance automatically to compensate for the rocking motion of the deck. But when you first step off on to solid land you feel like you're still rocking and swaying.

Trampolines/bouncy castles

Bounce around for long enough and your brain starts to get the hang of it – bending and straightening your knees as your feet hit the canvas to keep your jumps high and light. But when you step off again your knees bend as you hit the solid, un-bouncy ground, and it feels like your legs weigh a ton!

Why does spinning make you dizzy?

Because your brain gets confused between what you're seeing and what you're feeling. The brain senses that you're spinning using special gravity-and-motion-sensing organs in your inner ear, which work together with your eyes to keep your vision and balance stable. But when you suddenly **stop** spinning the system goes haywire, and your brain thinks you're moving while you're not!

I have gravity and motion sensors in my ears? Why has no one told me that before?   Coooooool

Of course you do. How else could you know if you were moving, spinning or standing on your head, even with your eyes closed?

Hmmm. I hadn't thought about it like that. I always thought we just figured all that out by looking.

Well, of course vision plays a part in balance and movement too.

If you don't believe this, try standing on one leg for a minute with your eyes open, and then with your eyes closed.

But your brain receives input and information from both eyes and ears in order to figure out which way up you are, how you're currently moving and whether you're moving at all.

So what do these motion sensors look like? If you look in your ear, can you see them?

Errr . . . how would you go about looking in your own ear?

All right, then – someone else's ear.

Well, you still wouldn't be able to see much. Your organs of balance and motion – called the **vestibular organs** – are behind the eardrum, deep within the inner ear. They sit behind the snail-like hearing organ called the **cochlea**, just behind a cavity called the **vestibule**, from which the organs get their name.

This means 'entrance hall' in Latin.

127

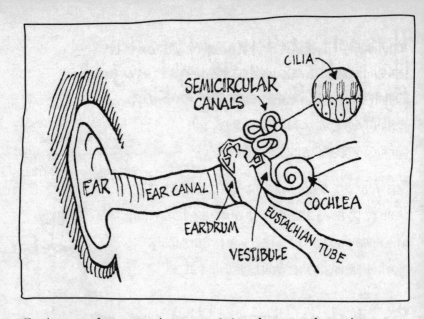

Each organ features three **semicircular canals** – three little loops or tubes that sit at different angles to each other so that they can sense both horizontal and vertical movements of the head. The inside of each canal is filled with a gloopy fluid called **endolymph** and lined with thousands of tiny hairs called **cilia**.

Now, here's the clever bit. The base of each hair is attached to a tiny branch of the vestibular nerve, which leads back to the brain. Every time you move, rotate or tilt your head, the gloopy endolymph liquid swishes within the semicircular canals, bending the cilia over like bits of seaweed in an ocean tide. Once bent, these little hairs send a signal to the brain, telling it how fast (and in what direction) your head is moving.

Together with a set of little gravity-sensing structures called **otoliths** (which sit just beside the semicircular canals), your vestibular organs can sense any type and direction of motion, and relay that information to the brain so that it can figure out:

a) your *orientation*, or which way up your body is, relative to the ground

b) your *linear acceleration*, or how fast you're moving in a given direction, and

c) your *angular acceleration*, or how fast and in which direction you're rotating or spinning

. . . and all this works even with your eyes closed. Your eyes just supply extra information, so that your brain can confirm what's going on. Pretty neat, eh?

Yeah, I s'pose so. But if it all works so well, then why do we sometimes feel like we're still spinning, even after we've stopped?

Ah, that's because of a temporary upset in your **vestibulo-ocular reflex**.

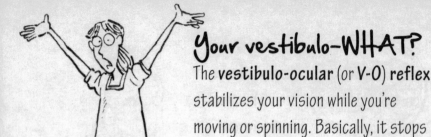

Your vestibulo-WHAT?

The **vestibulo-ocular** (or **V-O**) **reflex** stabilizes your vision while you're moving or spinning. Basically, it stops the world going blurry as it whizzes by in the opposite direction. It does this by sending information about how you're moving from the vestibular organs in the ears to the muscles that move the eyes. When your eye muscles receive this info, they respond by making lots of little rotating movements in the opposite direction to the way you're spinning. That way, your eyes can keep 'scanning' or 'scrolling' your surroundings, keeping them in focus even as they whizz past you.

Through nerves, of course. It wouldn't do much good if they had to telephone or email your eyeballs instead, would it?

Yes . . . we're still spinning . . .

This all works fine until you come to a sudden stop. When you stop spinning suddenly, your head and body stop moving, but the fluid in your semicircular canals keeps sloshing around, and it takes a while for the bent-over cilia to right themselves and stop sending 'I'm spinning' signals to the eye muscles. So the eyes just do what they're told, and they keep scrolling backwards to compensate for the spin. This makes it seem as if the whole world is still wheeling around you (in the opposite direction to the way you were just spinning), even though you're standing or sitting quite still!

Whoooaaaa!

Crazy. But then why does that make you fall over or feel sick?

If you're standing or sitting straight, with your head vertical and upright, it doesn't. Within ten to twenty seconds your brain figures out what's going on, the spinning sensation stops, and you're fine. But if you tilt your head off-centre — by leaning backwards, forward or off to one side — *that's* when the problems start.

Assuming you're spinning off-centre like an out-of-control figure skater, your brain attempts to correct your posture — shifting the alignment of your knees, hips and spine to bring you upright again. But since you're not *actually spinning at all* this does no good whatsoever! Instead, it makes you lean and teeter off balance and (very probably) fall to the ground in a confused heap.

The mismatch between the info your brain is getting from the ears and what it can see with your eyes may cause **motion sickness**, which is what makes you feel queasy and ill.

Experiment:
You Spin Me (Right Round)

Ready to dizzy it up for yourself? Take care, stay safe and don't do these so long that you make yourself sick. But give them a quick try, and feel for yourself how your balance organs work.

1 Grab a short stick, put one end to the ground, and run in a circle round that point ten to twelve times. Now stop quickly, drop the stick and try to walk in a straight line. How'd it go?

2 Now sit on a swivelling chair and get a friend to spin you round quickly, ten to twelve times, then stop you suddenly. How does that feel? Any different?

3 Now repeat the experiment above, but close your eyes. Open them once you stop. How was that? Room still spinning, or not?

4 Finally, repeat the experiment once more, this time with your head tilted *slightly* to one side during the spin. Feel better or worse?

Read through the previous chapter again, and see if you can figure out what's happening in your ears, eyes and brain to make you dizzy.

Get It Sorted – The Brain

You can divide the brain into **three** basic layers. The deepest is the **brainstem**, which is essentially the top end of your spinal cord plus a small bulge that sits on top. Wrapped around that, like a fleshy peach around its stone, is the brain region that contains the **limbic system**. Outside that is the **neocortex**. The name, in Latin, means 'new shell'. And that's pretty much what it looks like – a thick, wrinkly nutshell that covers the inner regions of the brain. This region is only fully developed in humans and other higher mammals.

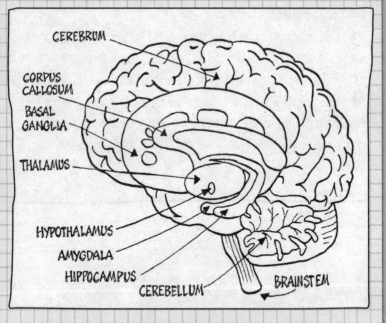

The **brainstem** is responsible for creating the most primitive emotional reactions or reflexes. These include fear or aggression in response to pain, and happiness (or relief) at finding safety or food.

The **limbic system** contains several different brain regions, each with its own role in creating emotions. This is where most of our basic emotions come from. It includes:

The **Amygdala** – This controls fear, rage and aggression.

The **Hippocampus** – This is involved in the formation of learned emotions or emotional memories. If this region is damaged, you can't retain any new memories at all. So even if you were terrified by a snake attack once before, without a working hippocampus, you wouldn't remember what it felt like (so wouldn't be afraid of snakes) the next time you encountered one.

The **Thalamus** and **Hypothalamus** – These regions create desires that help you to regulate the body, such as hunger and thirst.

Finally, outside the brainstem and limbic system, the **neocortex** helps create more complex emotions like hope, joy, love, sadness, disgust and despair. This region of the brain is only fully developed in humans. So while other intelligent mammals may also experience these emotions, they don't feel them the same way we do.

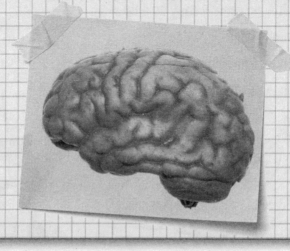

Could you live with half a brain?

Yes, you could! Your brain is divided into two halves that mirror each other in shape, size and function. And while each half does have its specialities, you could survive and learn to use just one half if the other was damaged or removed.

Your brain really has two halves? Like, you could fit your fingers in between them?

Yes, it really does. The two halves (or hemispheres) of the brain sit together in the skull, and are tethered by a cluster of nerves and blood vessels called the **corpus callosum**. Even with this holding the hemispheres together, the gap between them is big enough to slip your fingers into once the brain is outside the body (trust me — I've done it). **Eeeeewwww!**

And it's extremely easy to snip through these fleshy tethers and fold the hemisphere apart like two halves of an apple.

Actually, it looks a lot more like a cauliflower. And it's about the same size and weight as a bunch of bananas. But you get the idea.

But why would the brain come in two bits? Why not just one big lump of stuff – like your heart or your liver?

Because human bodies – like those of fish, birds, reptiles and most other animals – are largely symmetrical. This means that you could chop a human body in half lengthways, and the left half would be a mirror image (more or less) of the right half. This is because of the way our bodies grow and develop.

On the journey from egg to embryo, we start out as a single egg. This turns into a ball of cells, which in turn lengthens out to become a flattened tube – with a head (or mouth) end, tail (or bottom) end, a front, a back, a left side and a right side. Later, as the limbs and organs develop within this body, every limb or organ (with very few exceptions) that appears on the left side is mirrored by an identical one on the right.

This is why you have two arms, two legs, two eyes, two ears and two nostrils. And, of course, these paired organs aren't just limited to the ones you can see on the outside. Inside the body, you have two lungs, two kidneys and two ovaries (if you're a girl) or two testicles (if you're a boy).

But what about your mouth, your bottom, your heart and your liver? You don't have two of those, do you?

You only have *one* mouth and *one* bottom because these form at opposite ends of the embryo while it's still a tube — *before* the embryo develops left and right 'sides'.

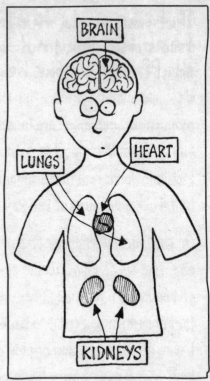

(If they formed later, you might end up with two bottoms. Just think how weird that would be.)

Other digestive organs, like the liver, pancreas, appendix, small intestine and large intestine, form as offshoots of this 'mouth-to-bottom' tube. So they don't obey the left/right rule either. And while the heart *does* end up sitting slightly to one side of the centre of the chest, it actually forms in two halves – the left and right **ventricles** – separated by a septum in the middle. And, although the left one is a little bigger, we can say that the basic structure of the heart is symmetrical too.

And that's how it is with the brain. Like the heart, it isn't quite symmetrical, and the two halves don't work independently – they work together to order information from sensory nerves, and to produce thoughts, speech and movement via motor nerves. But in a way, the two hemispheres of the brain are like your lungs, your kidneys or the other 'paired' organs in the body. Because if you lose or damage one of them, the other can take up the slack and keep you alive.

Seriously? I mean, I guess I've heard of someone losing a kidney or lung and surviving. But living with half your brain?

Yep. It's rare, but it happens. If you lose or damage a **kidney**, the other one grows by up to 50 per cent in order to take on the extra work of filtering your blood. If you lose or damage a **lung**, there's little room for the remaining lung to grow, but if it's healthy it'll do its job well enough for you to survive. And in some rare cases people with

Actually, a good number of people are born with just one kidney in the first place, due to birth defects. But, because the remaining one does its job so well, they may never know they have just one until they're X-rayed!

brain conditions such as epilepsy have to have the connection between the two halves of their **brain** severed, or have an entire half of the brain removed altogether.

When this happens, fluid fills the space left behind, and it may leave the patient temporarily unable to speak or move properly. But within a year the speaking and moving functions previously handled by the missing half are taken over by the half that remains. And, believe it or not, this works well enough for the patient to live a full lifetime (although they might still suffer with some physical or mental disabilities) with — literally — half a brain.

But if you can survive with only half a brain, what do you need the other half for?

Well, while the two halves of the brain are similar, and can take over from each other if need be, they're not identical. Each half specializes in certain types of task.

The **left side** of the brain handles more of the reasoning and mathematical calculation, and enables you to understand grammar and recognize words when you learn a language. If certain parts of your left hemisphere are damaged, you become unable to speak or form words.

The **right side** is used more in interpreting the *sounds* and *emotions* of language and speech. It is used more in listening to music. And it also deals better with visual information, like recognizing faces and facial expressions.

But while the two sides of your brain may specialize in slightly different things, what's really important is how they work together and complement each other. But as we've already learned, if you only have one half left to work with, your brain can still make do. It just takes time for the brain to rewire itself, so that it can handle most or all of the jobs it was doing before.

So when my teacher tells me to 'use my brain', can I ask her which half?

Well, you could try it. But nobody likes a smarty-pants. Even one with half a brain . . .

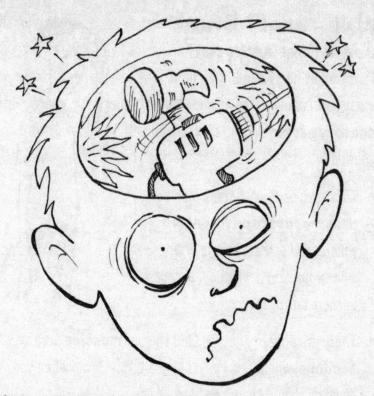

What happens in your head during a headache?

That depends on what's causing it. Headaches can be caused by any number of different things going on inside your bonce — including pinched nerves, tight blood vessels and swollen brain membranes. But, while your brain *receives and interprets pain signals*, it can't actually feel pain at all. Brain pain is a funny thing . . .

Wait – what? Brains don't feel any pain?

That's right, they don't. For the most part, pain starts at the tips of **sensory nerves** spread throughout your body.

- There are sensory nerves tied to **pain receptors** on your **skin**, which send signals to the brain when your skin is pinched, scraped, burned, cut or pierced.

- There are sensory nerves tied to your **muscles** and **tendons**, which send pain signals to the brain when you stretch or pull them too hard.

- There are sensory nerves running alongside **blood vessels** throughout your body, which send pain signals to the brain when your **tissues** and **organs** are bumped, squashed, cut or punctured.

But the *inside* of the brain itself contains no sensory nerve endings at all. So it can't feel any pain. None at all. In fact, when brain surgeons operate on tumours and brain lesions, they sometimes leave the patient awake while they do it!

Yikes! Really?

Yep, it's true. Since cutting through the skin and skull *would be* painful, the patient is usually given a local anaesthetic to kill the pain at the surface. But once the 'lid' is off (so to speak), the surgeon can slice and dice away at the brain itself while *chatting* to the wide-awake patient!

FREAKY!!

Okay, so if headaches don't actually happen inside your brain, then why does it FEEL like they do?

Because the cause of the headache is often still inside your *head* — just not inside the brain itself. Your brain, after all, isn't the only thing inside your skull. Between your brain and your skull, there are three layers of fatty membranes called **meninges** (these are the things that get infected if you have **meningitis**).

The average brain is about 60 per cent fat, with most of the rest being water.

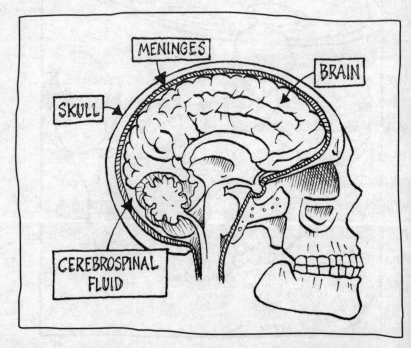

SKULL

MENINGES

BRAIN

CEREBROSPINAL FLUID

They contain a vast web of blood vessels which brings oxygen and nutrients to the hungry brain below, and envelop the brain in a protective triple-bag of fat and **cerebrospinal fluid**. (Picture a grey, fatty lasagne on top of your cauliflower-like brain and you're not far off.)

Anyway, it's these *surrounding* areas — not the brain itself — that are most often the cause of headaches. Most often, headaches are caused by pinched or narrowed blood vessels within the meninges. As the blood pressure builds up behind the pinch, the vessel walls get stretched, and pain receptors in the walls signal the brain to say there's a problem.

But what makes that happen? I mean, if headaches are so common, those blood vessels must get pinched all the time, right?

Well, there are over **100,000 miles** of blood vessels surrounding the brain (enough, if you unwound them all, to wrap right round the Earth four times!). So there's plenty of room for pinches and swellings to happen *somewhere* in there. And there are *lots* of different ways they can get pinched and swollen.

Like what?

The simplest way is if you **bump your head**. Do this hard enough, and it will crush or bust open small blood vessels surrounding the brain, causing a painful headache. (Bust or crush enough of them, and you can end up with brain damage – all the more reason to wear a helmet if you're on a bike or skateboard.)

If you don't drink enough water and become **dehydrated**, an entire membrane can shrink as it loses water, squeezing blood vessels inside and causing another type of headache. On the flipside, if you drink too much water (which is called **hyperhydration**), your whole brain can swell up and press against the membranes, causing yet another type of headache.

Other common causes for headaches include:

1 Pulled or stiff neck muscles – these pinch nerves and blood vessels in the back of the head.

2 Eye strain – nerve pain from overworked muscles that control your eye movements. Again, these nerves are close enough to the brain for it to confuse it with 'brain pain'.

3 Respiratory and sinus infections – the viruses that cause colds, flu and other respiratory diseases can infect your nasal passages and sinuses, causing swelling of the membranes inside. These then press on nerves and blood vessels behind the eyes, nose and forehead, causing painful 'pressure' or 'sinus' headaches until the infection is fought off.

4 Alcohol, drugs, medicines, stress, air pressure changes and allergies to certain foods, all of which cause swelling in the blood vessels of the meninges.

5 . . . And, of course, sudden heat loss from the roof of the mouth caused by eating frozen foods too fast – which causes the nerves above to shrink up. This gives a lovely 'behind-the-eye' headache . . . better known as **BRAIN FREEZE** or **ICE-CREAM HEADACHE!**

Experiment: Send More Blood to Your Brain!

No, I'm not going to make you stand on your head. This is all about showing how your brain demands more blood flow (to get more glucose and oxygen) the more you put it to work.

Remember the heartbeat experiment back on page 48? Well this time, you're going to find the heartbeat in your throat, in one of the main arteries leading to the brain. Here's how you do it:

1 Place two fingers (lightly) along the side of your throat, just beneath the jaw and to one side of the middle. Press down gently until you feel your pulse beating in the artery beneath.

2 Relax, and measure your heartbeats per minute using a stopwatch (or get a friend to time it while you count beats), just as we did before. Note the number down.

3 Now get your friend to place his fingers on your throat, in the same place you had yours. Once they've checked they can feel it, have them start the timer and count how many times your pulse beats for you.

4 In that one minute, try to think of as many different animal species as you can – cats, dogs, iguanas, ostriches – you name it. Even dinosaurs, if you like. Just keep going, and see if you can think of at least thirty of them. Don't stop thinking!

5 Now have your friend tell you what your heart rate for that frantic thinking minute was. Compare it with the 'resting, relaxed' rate from before. Chances are it was much higher the second time, as thinking hard actually redirects blood to your hungry brain! Believe it or not, thinking is *hard* work!

ANSWERS

Page 35: Blood-clot Boggle

The right order is C, A, D, E, B

Page 68: Diet and Digestion Wordsearch

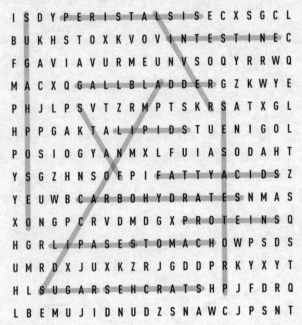

Page 106: Bendy Bones

The chicken bone becomes very bendy and flexible, almost like rubber! This is because you used the vinegar (otherwise known as acetic acid) to dissolve away all the chalky minerals that gave the bone its hardness, leaving only the rubbery, gel-like tissue behind. Nice work!

Picture Credits

SPACE

THE WHOLE WHIZZ-BANG STORY

WHAT IS THE UNIVERSE?
WHAT WOULD HAPPEN IF YOU WERE FLYING
A SPACESHIP NEAR A BLACK HOLE?
HOW DO WE KNOW THAT STARS AND GALAXIES
ARE BILLIONS OF YEARS OLD?

GLENN MURPHY ANSWERS THESE AND A LOT OF OTHER BRILLIANT
QUESTIONS IN THIS FUNNY AND INFORMATIVE BOOK.

PACKED WITH INFORMATION, PUZZLES, QUIZZES, PHOTOS
AND DOODLES ABOUT ALL SORTS OF INCREDIBLE THINGS
LIKE SUPERMASSIVE BLACK HOLES, GALAXIES, TELESCOPES,
PLANETS, SOLAR FLARES, CONSTELLATIONS, ECLIPSES AND RED
DWARFS, THIS BOOK HAS NO BORING BITS!

By me,
GLENN MURPHY

DISGUSTING SCIENCE

WHAT'S WORSE THAN FINDING A MAGGOT IN YOUR APPLE?
WHICH SMELLS WORSE: A ROTTEN EGG OR A ROTTEN LEG?
WHAT ARE SICK AND POO MADE OF?

GLENN MURPHY, AUTHOR OF WHY IS SNOT GREEN?,
ANSWERS THESE AND LOTS OF OTHER REVOLTING QUESTIONS
IN THIS HILARIOUS, FASCINATING AND INFORMATIVE BOOK.

PACKED WITH ILLUSTRATIONS, PHOTOGRAPHS AND FACTS
ABOUT ALL SORTS OF DISGUSTING THINGS, FROM BUGS,
BACTERIA AND SWEATY ARMPITS TO EXPLODING BODIES
AND CREEPY-CRAWLY CREATURES, THIS BOOK CONTAINS
ABSOLUTELY NO BORING BITS!

GLENN MURPHY